An Authentic American History

PURITANS'

A CATHOLIC PERSPECTIVE

PROGRESS

VOLUME
5

COMPILED BY THE EDITORS
OF ANGELUS PRESS
MATTHEW ANGER
PETER CHOJNOWSKI, PH.D.
MICHAEL MANCUSO
REV. FR. KENNETH NOVAK

1942–1969
Determining the Future

ANGELUS PRESS
2918 TRACY AVENUE, KANSAS CITY, MISSOURI 64109

ANGELUS PRESS

2918 TRACY AVENUE
KANSAS CITY, MISSOURI 64109
PHONE (816) 753-3150
FAX (816) 753-3557
ORDER LINE 1-800-966-7337

ISBN   0-935952-35-7 Series
       0-935952-40-3 Volume 5

FIRST PRINTING—February 1996

Printed in the United States of America

CONTENTS

WORLD WAR AND COLD WAR
1942-1951

WAR AT LAST

On November 19, 1941, the Japanese Foreign Ministry informed its embassy in Washington that if war with the United States was imminent, it would have broadcast over Tokyo's radio station JAP the weather report, "east wind rain." Since the US military and naval intelligence had previously cracked the Japanese codes, this was known immediately to FDR. Armed forces receiving stations were put on the alert for just such a message.

As we have seen, Secretary of State Hull had rejected Japanese peace terms on November 26, demanding immediate withdrawal of all Japanese forces immediately from China and French Indo-China. This ultimatum was obviously impossible to comply with, and on December 4, the east wind message was duly broadcast. Those who intercepted it, a Lieutenant Commander Kramer and a Commander Stafford, reported it to their superior, Rear Admiral Noyes, who in turn passed it on to the President's naval aide. There can be no doubt that Roosevelt was aware that the Japanese intended to commence hostilities.

The historical consensus, however, is that FDR imagined that such an assault would commence in the Philippines and the Dutch East Indies; according to the *Encyclopedia Britanica*, he was quite surprised when the attack came upon Hawaii.

If that is so, of course, it would simply show the duplicity of FDR's dealing with the American people; the America First Committee had charged repeatedly that Roosevelt wanted to get this nation into the war by hook or by crook. It is, as we saw, a matter of record that when approached on several occasions by the Japanese to negotiate, his administration refused. Thus it is obvious that despite his promises to the American people, Roosevelt was willing to waste the lives of American boys in pursuance of a policy the American people did not want. Call it what you will, this cannot be said to be either democracy or honesty.

There is, however, evidence to suggest that Roosevelt did know that an attack on Pearl Harbor was imminent. For example, having cracked the Japanese codes the Navy Department was in a position to track Japanese naval moves. Moreover, although the old and obsolete battleships were left at Pearl Harbor, ships which would have been little use in modern war (which FDR would have known, having been Assistant Secretary of the Navy in the First World War), the aircraft carriers were sent out to sea and so escaped destruction. There is more. Speaking of the intercepted east wind rain message, Charles Tansill declares:

> It would be ordinarily assumed that the President, after reading this intercepted message, would hurriedly call a conference of the more important Army and Navy officers to concert plans to meet the anticipated attack. The testimony of General Marshall and Admiral Stark would indicate that he made no effort to consult with them. Did he deliberately seek the Pearl Harbor attack

in order to get America into the war? What is the real answer to this riddle of Presidential composure in the face of a threatened attack upon some American outpost in the faraway Pacific? The problem grows more complicated as we approach zero hour. At 9:00am [Eastern time] on December 7, Lieutenant Commander Kramer delivered to Admiral Stark the final installment of the Japanese instruction to [their Ambassador] Nomura. Its meaning was now so obvious that Stark cried out in great alarm: "My God! This means war. I must get word to [commanding officer at Pearl, Admiral] Kimmel at once." But he made no effort to contact Honolulu. Instead, he tried to get in touch with General Marshall, who for some strange reason, suddenly decided to go on a long horseback ride. It was a history-making ride....In the early hours of World War II, General Marshall took a ride that helped prevent an alert from reaching Pearl Harbor in time to save an American fleet from serious disaster and an American garrison from a bombing that cost more than 2,000 lives. Was there an important purpose behind this ride?...

When Colonel Bratton, on the morning of December 7, saw the last part of the Japanese instruction to Nomura he realized that "Japan planned to attack the United States at some point at or near 1 o'clock that day." To Lieutenant Commander Kramer the message meant "surprise attack at Pearl Harbor today." This information was in the hands of Secretary [of War] Knox by 10:00am, and he must have passed it on to the President immediately.

It was 11:25am when General Marshall returned to his office. If he carefully read the reports on the threatened Japanese attack (on Pearl Harbor) he still had plenty of time to contact Honolulu by means of the scrambler telephone on his desk, or by the Navy radio or the FBI radio. For some reason best known to himself he chose to send the alert to Honolulu by RCA and did not even take the precaution to have it stamped "priority." As the Army Pearl Harbor Board significantly remarked: "We find no justification for a failure to send this message by multiple secret means either through the Navy radio or the FBI radio or the scrambler telephone or all three." Was the General under Presidential orders to break military regulations with regard to the transmission of important military information? (*Back Door to War*, pp.651-652).

If Professor Tansill's inference is correct, then FDR knowingly sacrificed over 2,000 American lives at Pearl Harbor to involve the country in a war which otherwise he could never have managed to get the country into. Had FDR alerted the Japanese to his knowledge of their actions; had he dispatched the navy to interdict them on the high seas; in a word, had he either convinced them to desist, or else defeated them with a minimal loss of American life, it would have been impossible to interest Americans in another war. In the words of then-House Majority Leader John W. McCormack: "We couldn't get a declaration of war through Congress. If Pearl Harbor hadn't happened, in my opinion the intense isolationism was so strong, we never would have entered the war" (Roy Hoopes, *Americans Remember the Home Front,* p.23). Obviously, had FDR negotiated a settlement with Japanese before they felt forced into war, this would have been doubly true. The course of Japanese actions had been predicted decades before by widely-known American military analyst, Homer Lea.

As it was, the assault fell upon an utterly unprepared Pearl Harbor; the surprise was perfect. Admiral Kimmel's reputation would be ruined for not being better prepared, though obviously he was a scapegoat. Over 2,000 Americans died, including the band of the USS Arizona; having won a battle of the bands in a Honolulu hotel the night before, they were permitted to sleep in the morning of December 7. So they shall until the last trump when the earth opens up its graves.

The effect was all FDR could possibly have hoped for. The America Firsters, until now rigidly opposed to a war which did not concern this country, jumped to the colors when, as they thought, the Japanese made a totally unprovoked sneak attack. The President's stirring speech to Congress is impressed to this day on our national consciousness: "Yesterday, December Seventh, 1941, a date which shall live in infamy..." As soon as the news reached the various parts of the country, crowds formed in various areas, including Lafayette Square by the White House. Hymns were sung in churches, and the first blackouts engulfed America. Fear was especially widespread on the West Coast.

Immediately, long-prepared defense plans went into effect: soldiers, sailors, police, and newly mobilized civilian guards were set to guarding dams, bridges, reservoirs, and the like. Censorship too went into effect, with all cables, letters, and radiograms being sent out of the country made subject to scrutiny. All over America, young men rushed to enlist, while even 81-year-old General "Black Jack" Pershing hobbled on his cane from Walter Reed Medical Center to the White House to offer his services to FDR.

Even more, perhaps, than in 1917, America's entrance into the War in 1941 reflected the European experience in 1914. Unlike that first conflict, when there was no question of foreign invasion, on this occasion there might be. While few mobilized in 1917 actually saw service in the AEF, many thousands of American young people would in the course of this war be transported all over the world; moreover, they would not come back when it was "over, over there" as their fathers had, but would remain even unto this day, as the world's policemen. For Europe, the old order ended in 1914; for us, it was really 1941.

On December 11, war was declared on Japan's allies, Germany and Italy. Roosevelt's primary interest was thus served. But events in the Far East pushed Europe out of the popular mind. The day before, Guam had fallen to the Japanese; little Wake would hold out gallantly until December 22. In the meantime, the Japanese invasion of the Philippines was in full swing. Heavily outnumbered, the American and Filipino defenders of the island of Luzon were pushed steadily back toward their prepared final redoubts of the Bataan Peninsula and Corrigidor.

We will rejoin our forces overseas before long. For now, let us focus on the home front. Almost immediately, automobile production was shut down; General Motors was the last to do so, in early February, 1942. At sea American shipping was in great danger from both German and Japanese subs; this danger soon extended to the coast itself. On February 23, a Japanese midget sub lobbed shells at an oil refinery west of Santa Barbara, California (they missed their target, but did manage to stampede a herd of nearby horses). Two nights later, at 2:25 in the morning, the civil defense of Los Angeles blacked out the city, air-raid sirens wailed, anti-aircraft guns fired, and searchlights broke the night.

All for nothing. Despite the widespread pandemonium in the streets (including many auto accidents) caused by the black-out, despite the furor and rushing around, the celebrated "Battle of Los Angeles" was a real non-event, caused by war fever and mass hysteria. The only damage caused by weaponry was that to windows and roofs hit by anti-aircraft shrapnel. Western Defense Command insisted that there had been unfriendly aircraft about, but to this day none has ever been identified by any other source.

Amusing as this incident may seem, it had one terribly

serious result: all Japanese-Americans were removed from their homes on the West Coast, from Seattle to San Diego, and placed in detention camps. They were forced to leave all at once, and to leave most of their belongings behind; in hours, one of the most hard-working ethnic groups in America were reduced to absolute penury. Unlike German and Italian Americans, no Japanese American was ever convicted of spying for the enemy: indeed, Japanese Americans were instrumental in cracking the Japanese codes. While their elders, wives, and younger siblings languished in camps like Manzanar and Tule Lake, the youthful Japanese of the 442nd Regimental Combat Team fought in Europe and became the most highly decorated American unit of World War II. This disgraceful action was all the more ironic because approved by California Governor Earl Warren, whom we shall meet again in the next chapter as a great Liberal.

Civil Defense organizations blossomed everywhere; an Arts Council was formed to mobilize actors, writers, and artists behind the war effort. Melvyn Douglas was appointed by Eleanor Roosevelt to head it. Just as with the New Deal, so too, the Roosevelts saw the war effort as a cause to further centralize American life under government direction. As head of the Office of Civil Defense, Mrs. Roosevelt was able to indulge all her interests. One was physical fitness, for which she hired John B. Kelly (father of Grace Kelly, noted actress who became Princess Grace of Monaco), former Olympic sculling champion, as head of the PF program.

Dancing particularly enthralled the First Lady:

> She proclaimed a "Dance-for-Health Week" that would commence on April third. Then the First Lady set an example by organizing folk dances during coffee breaks and lunch hours in the enameled corridors of OCD headquarters. This was a commandeered apartment building on Dupont Circle, bordering "Embassy Row." She

not only arranged the dances; she often led them" (A.A. Hoehling, *Home Front, USA.,* pp.38-39).

Amusing as these capers were, the torrent of ridicule they and other of her activities provoked led eventually to Mrs. Roosevelt's resignation.

Her replacement, former Harvard Law Dean James Landis met a similar fate. Civil defense hysteria was such that, despite the fact that neither Germans nor Japanese possessed bombers capable of reaching the continental US, Landis ordered teams of emergency fire fighters trained everywhere, just in case.

A seemingly never-ending cornucopia of civil defense schemes poured from Landis' mind. But:

> The "block plan" was to prove Landis' Waterloo. The catastrophe was not especially surprising since the block warden was heaped with duties and prerogatives which far exceeded his normal role. In addition to calling attention to offending lights or reminding that air-raid drills were in progress, he or she was supposed to encourage housewives to save fats, conserve sugar, help draw up car pools, provide the counsel of a veteran agronomist on the culture of victory gardens, and even boom the WAVES and WACS to eligible females.
>
> To many legislators, especially Republicans, these wardens appeared to be the American equivalent of block "fuehrers," or leaders, in Nazi-governed towns and cities. The wardens seemed to be assuming an ever-encroaching role in the nation's home life, barely stopping short of changing the diapers of the block's infants. Alarmists feared their next step would be to call the political tune for their captive wards (Hoehling, *op. cit.,* pp.44-45).

The scheme was stopped, and in the spring of 1944 the OCD was abolished. But "alarmists" had reason to be alarmed. Although the Communists had always been present in the New Deal, and while, during the period of the pact between Germany and the Soviet Union they had been loud pacifists, Hitler's invasion of Russia caused them once again to support the pro-war forces. Once we were in, Communist actors, writers, directors, and so on became very powerful in Hollywood, lending their efforts to propaganda films like *Mission to Moscow*. Since Stalin was our ally, the doings of Communists in this country went unchecked and even were tacitly fostered in certain areas by government representatives. In Hollywood, this took the form of an unofficial black list, whereby outspoken anti-Communist film-folk found it difficult to find work during the war. They would remember this afterwards.

More frightening still, however, was the government's use of the emergency to increase its stranglehold on the economy and on political life. The former resulted from a simple fact: war materiel had to be produced. After Pearl Harbor, 20,000 of our best warplanes were shipped to Great Britain and the Soviet Union. Tanks and planes must be turned out to replace them, as well as rifles, oil, military posts, and everything concerning the conflict. Old factories must be converted, new ones built, and housing for workers provided. One result of this and the draft was the immediate dissolution of the Great Depression and the country's unemployment problem; the second was the inauguration in January 1942 of the all-powerful War Production Board. The WPB, working hand in glove with the Justice Department could requisition the entire output of any mine or factory, and direct its use and allocation. To build up the labor pool, convicts were used, aliens given work permits, and above all, women were put to work, as in World War I. But this time, the ladies labored in much larger numbers. This, together with the formation of the first large industrial suburbs be-

gan two major social changes which would bear fruit after
the war: the flight of American women from the home to
the workplace, and the flight of the middle class from the
cities to the suburbs. This latter would have the effect of
increasing housing at the expense of the environment while
at the same time spelling the death of the inner cities. Moreover, the creation of such new and artificial towns and cities
would have the effect of cutting large numbers of Americans
off even further from any of their past traditions.

Like unto the WPB was the Office of Price Administration. Headed by Leon Henderson, the OPA took charge of
rationing, which began in March of 1942. Initially, only sugar
was rationed, but in quick succession shoes, coffee, gasoline,
rubber and butter followed. Much of these were sent to sus-
tain our allies. Occasionally the uses they were put to were
intriguing: Russians, for example, unused to butter, employed
it to grease rifles and other things. More and more items,
from radios to car parts to paper to toys became rationed or
scarce. Much of this was to be expected, as the needs of the
war consumed an ever-increasing share of production. But,
at least as far as the OPA was concerned, there was more
involved. "Controls, [Henderson] declared, should be yet
tighter and extend to still more commodities. Underlying
much of his philosophy and his efforts was a desire, repeatedly avowed in public by Henderson, to level out society
more equally. He alluded to the change in rich homes and
habits, especially the anticipated extinction of the multi-ser-
vant household" (Hoehling, *op. cit.*, p.66).

Although this latter did indeed occur for the most part
(though such places as the White House and the Roosevelt
estate at Hyde Park were exempted) Henderson's officious-
ness resulted in his forced resignation in 1943. His policies
continued however, resulting in (among other things) the
virtual death of the multiservant estate–a noteworthy loss

since it meant the passage of a certain style of life. Amy
Vanderbilt describes this in her *Etiquette:*

> The day of the complete staff, of formal entertain-
> ment, except in a limited way, is about done. The most
> exclusive men's tailors in the country say they have no
> ready-made liveries any more because there are no longer
> customers to support the department. The very few es-
> tablishments with permanent men servants must have
> liveries made to order.
>
> This is the day of the electric dishwasher, the storage
> wall, the dining ell, the deep freeze, buffet meals, day
> workers, cleaning services by the hour, unionized bonded
> help, sitters, the automatic washing machine, the dryer,
> and nursery school instead of Nanny (p.476).
>
> Most of us do our own work or make do with occa-
> sional or regular part-time help as I've said above. There
> are indeed, however, some households run with full staff,
> which have some of the facilities still for the kind of gra-
> cious living once quite usual among those who could
> afford it....
>
> Most of us don't want to live this way any more even
> if it were possible (p.504).

While Miss Vanderbilt may not have wished so to live,
and indeed, while today's American wealthy might for the
most part echo her sentiments, it is truly unfortunate for
them as well as for the rest of us. As you may remember
from earlier on, it is in fact the landed gentry, with their
tenants and staffs of servants, who acted as this country's
first governing class. Were they good or bad, they learned
from dealing with servants to look beyond their own interests, and to deal on a small scale in the little communities
which their homes were, with the problems which afflicted
town, province or state, and finally nation. In a word, their
experience as paternal employers assisted them in the leader-

ship role their wealth brought them. Today, such folk remain wealthy, and others have become rich; but the idea that wealth has a social use is foreign to them.

Moreover, since such folk were large scale employers in the areas where they lived, they both provided an incentive for local people (whether servants or simply outside suppliers of such households) to remain in rural areas, and carried much weight in local affairs. There they provided something of a counter to the centralizing tendencies of the Federal government. Although non-Catholic for the most part, to the degree that they could in their cloudy way, they attempted to fulfill the classic role of aristocracy as outlined by Pius XII in his Allocution to the Roman Nobility of January 16, 1946:

> As history will testify, wherever true democracy reigns, the life of the people is permeated with sound traditions, which it is not legitimate to destroy. The primary representatives of these traditions are the ruling classes, or rather, the groups of men and women, or the associations, which set the tone, as we say, for the village or the city, for the region or the entire country.

Whence the existence and influence, among all civilized peoples, of aristocratic institutions...

While such folk , being non-Catholic, had never functioned to the greatest possible good, they yet remained a tenuous connection with old Christendom. Moreover, they served to fulfill in some degree a function which Pius XII in the same allocution declared belonged to such folk:

> [T]hat of acting for the people, in all the facets of public life to which you might be called, as living examples of an unwavering performance of duty, as impartial, disinterested men who, free of all inordinate lust for success or wealth, do not accept a post except to serve the good cause, courageous men unafraid of losing favor from above, or of threats from below.

He had already said to the same audience in an Allocution of January 14, 1945 that the excellence their state in life required would be:

> [M]ade manifest in the dignity of one's entire bearing and conduct—a dignity that is not imperious, however, and that, far from emphasizing distances, only lets them appear when necessary to inspire in others a higher nobility of soul, mind, and heart.

In a secularized (and so less effective way) these values were aspired to by the class that the OPA set on its way to extinction. As was said of the founder of the Hotchkiss School, a favored prep school for such folk:

> Though he never came right out and said so, George Van Santvoord was emphasizing the true standards of a true aristocracy—standards of cultivation, of intellect, of duty, of generosity of spirit, standards of doing one's best. The fact is that out of schools like Groton and Hotchkiss, out of even the most hothouse-seeming notions of how the children of the American rich should be educated, would emerge people who, when the chips were down, would manage to rise to occasions and do the things that were expected of them (Stephen Birmingham, *America's Secret Aristocracy*, p.253).

So they rose, for better or worse, in every one of this nation's conflicts. World War II would be their last major war. Their descendants exist still, and some retain their traditions. But there is now no hope of them being a force around which opposition to the regime in power might coalesce. Today the citizenry of this country tolerate things their ancestors would not have; part of the reason for this is the lack of effective leadership—a lack in no small part due to the erosion of the class which once provided it. But because this class had, since the Revolution and the Civil War been consecrated to the ideals of Americanism, there was little they could do when effectively liquidated in the name of that ideology.

All that has been said in regard to the gathering of power in the hands of government might be dismissed as the natural growth of modern government. We have come to accept the notion that, so long as government is "nice," it has a right to all the power necessary to run the country. The idea that a people might run themselves has become foreign. But even under the new scheme of things, most folk would, one supposes, believe that even a modern state has no right to suppress peaceful opposition. But the wartime regime presided over by FDR did just that.

Among other things, the war gave Roosevelt the chance to even old scores. Thus, when Montgomery Ward was plagued by labor disputes, the opportunity was seized by the government to take control of the chain from board chairman and long-time FDR opponent Sewell Avery. In April 1944, Attorney General Biddle flew to Chicago with six helmeted soldiers. On April 26 at 10am, they arrived at Avery's office. When he refused to leave they carried him out bodily in his chair and deposited the 71-year-old on the sidewalk outside.

In Detroit, the new Archbishop, Francis Mooney, a friend of FDR's, silenced Fr. Coughlin and ended the publication of *Social Justice*. In this way, much that befell other opponents of the New Deal was spared the priest.

As noted earlier, there were a number of Italian and German Americans who spied for their former home-countries. The government took the opportunity, while ferreting out treason and traitors, to also discredit or imprison those whose crime was simply opposing the course which this country had taken since 1933. It will be readily admitted that there is a difference between taken a dissenting or even unpopular stand, and aiding and abetting the enemies of one's country.

Moreover, as we have seen in the case of natives of Communist countries who assisted our intelligence agencies against the regimes which oppressed their nations, even "treason" can appear justified to its practitioners on ideological grounds. If one is convinced of the evil nature of a regime, and for the sake of the country it rules aids that regime's foreign opponents, where does treason lie? We know that the Nazis and Communists were evil, indeed; but what of those who genuinely thought the same of Roosevelt? To this day we blithely do business with heirs of Mao Tse Tung, who was responsible for the deaths of tens of millions of Chinese, and spurn the successors of his opponents on Taiwan. Of what does our morality consist? As the saying has it:

> Treason never prospers;
> For if it prosper,
> None dare call it treason.

One might consider the subversion of a constitution to which a man has sworn allegiance to be treason; if this were true, then such a one might consider FDR a traitor. But in wartime, to think such thoughts would itself be called treason. Confusing, indeed.

On July 22, 1942, Attorney General Francis Biddle secured an indictment against twenty-eight defendants. Some were racists and indeed out and out Nazis, like William Dudley Pelley, leader of a group of would-be storm troopers called the "Silver Shirts." Others, like Prescott Freese Dennett, an avid America Firster who was well respected by a number of Congressmen and Senators, were quite respectable. But crackpot or respectable, the 28 were all accused by the indictment of treason:

> It being the plan and said purpose of said defendants,
> and divers other persons to the Grand Jurors unknown,

to destroy the morale and faith and confidence of the members of the military and naval forces of the United States and the people of the United States in their public officials and Republican form of government...

...the said defendants...planning and intending to seize upon and use and misuse the right of freedom of speech and of the press to spread their disloyal doctrines, intending and believing that any nation allowing to its people the right of freedom of speech and the press is powerless to defend itself against enemies masquerading as patriots and seeking to obstruct, impede, break down and destroy the proper functioning of its republican government under the guise of honest criticism...

One cannot help but wonder, given the present assurance that freedoms of speech and the press are absolute—particularly with regard to pornography and so on—if it was a tad disingenuous for the regime being criticized to determine whether that criticism was honest or not. In any case, the sought after convictions were achieved, as were those of many others. One of these was the aviatrix Laura Ingalls, who upon being found guilty declared:

Your honor, one of the great fundamentals implicit in our Constitution is liberty of conscience. I felt I had a right to follow the dictates of my conscience...I worked individually, and individualism is a real American trait. My motives were born of a burning patriotism and a high idealism...I am a truer patriot than those who convicted me...I salute the Republic of the United States!

With that she was led away. From April to November 1944, another 26 Americans were tried for sedition, including among their number anti-Catholic Gerald L.K. Smith and Catholic Elizabeth Dilling. Treason trials, like any other sort of politics, make strange bedfellows. In the end, the judge died on November 30, and a mistrial was declared. Had they been acquitted, it would have been a black day for FDR; had they been convicted, for America. As it was, little resulted.

Nevertheless, the struggle between the verbiage and the reality of the Americanist ideology was spelled out in detail. Later on, when the Vietnam war broke out, Americans opposed to it sometimes collaborated with the enemy in ways which would have won them prison during World War II. What had changed?

The War, in any case, altered America in much the same way that World War I changed Europe, despite the fact that we were not invaded. The rush of women to the work place helped destroy the notion of housewifery as a decent occupation. Relaxed morals led to a skyrocketing in the divorce rate, which has continued ever since. We have referred to the political consequences of the ruin of America's gentry. There were purely social ones as well. Where before the War, Americans aspired to "class," to dress and act with style, the emphasis on "democracy" and the demise of that class which formerly set standards replaced this aspiration with a taste for the casual. What was once considered male formal wear was seen less and less; in nightclubs and restaurants, the patrons gave up dinner jackets for suit-and-tie—eventually resulting in the curious fact that waiters were and are often better dressed than the clientele. Such relaxation was followed in etiquette, in speech, in a hundred things; taken up by movie actors, these trends accelerated.

Communism, as we have seen, spread in a sympathetic atmosphere. Such men as Harry Hopkins, the President's right hand man, and Alger Hiss, achieved high positions, and used them to help their cause. This would be a grave problem later.

In a nutshell, for all that we were on the winning side, the result on the Home Front was a defeat for all that was

best in the country. We shall now see the effect our intervention had on the world outside.

A WORLD AT WAR

Shortly after Pearl Harbor, Roosevelt and Churchill met
in Washington to coordinate the war effort. They agreed to
concentrate first on Europe, since, as Churchill put it, "It is
generally agreed that the defeat of Germany, entailing a collapse, will leave Japan exposed to overwhelming force, whereas
the defeat of Japan would not by any means bring the World
War to an end."

From the time that Britain and France had declared war
on Germany in response to Hitler's attack on Poland in September of 1939, the war had gone badly for the Allies there.
Poland fell swiftly, and then in 1940 Denmark, Norway, the
Netherlands, Belgium, and most surprising of all, France had
fallen to the seemingly invincible German army. The defeat
of these liberal democracies brought to the fore in each of
them internal divisions which had been brewing for a long
time.

In each, the Right wing was divided on how to deal with
the occupation, particularly since the invaders had had the
collaboration of the Communists (due to the Ribbentrop-
Molotov pact) in the invasion. How could one operate under German control? How true was the German rhetoric
about building a New Europe and an anti-Communist crusade? Did one trust the new rulers and work with them, or
did one work with leftists and with (after the invasion of the
Soviet Union in June 1941) the Communists in Resistance?
Not an easy call, indeed. In a word, with which despot would
you ally, Stalin or Hitler? Which could you trust?

The sovereigns, ruling and not, of Europe had obviously
little to hope for from the Communists; neither, however,

did they trust Hitler. The Archduke Otto von Habsburg, son of the saintly Charles I, had many supporters in both Austria and Hungary before the War. Both Dollfuss and his successor were in principle Monarchists. So much did Hitler fear a restoration that he named his planned invasion of Austria "Case Otto." But Otto was not restored, and the takeover was peaceful. When war began, Otto left for New York, and after Pearl Harbor was given charge of a Free Austrian battalion of 500 volunteers authorized by Secretary of War Stimson. But the outcry arising from anti-Monarchists in this country was great, and the battalion disbanded. So ended a chance for this nation to make some small reparation for the terrible wrong committed in our name by Woodrow Wilson.

In Germany itself, with few exceptions, the Royals had had little use for Hitler. The Kaiser himself, in exile in Holland, refused to acknowledge the Honor Guard sent to his home after the Germans conquered the country. His grandson and heir, Louis Ferdinand was briefly in the Army when the war started. Hitler, fearful that royal princes in the army showing heroism might win popularity, ordered all such gradually put out. Louis Ferdinand then involved himself casually with the plotters of July 20, 1944 (of whom more shortly) and had to go underground until the war ended. Crown Prince Rupert of Bavaria, an early foe of Hitler, saw his wife Crown Princess Antonia sent to Buchenwald concentration camp, where she was cruelly tortured; the Prince was forced into exile in Italy.

The heir to the Russian Imperial throne, Grand Duke Vladimir Cyrilovitch, lived in St. Brieuc, France, when the Germans conquered that country. Hitler offered the Grand Duke his throne if he would assist in the forthcoming invasion. He refused, and went to Spain.

Queen Wilhelmina of the Netherlands, King Haakon

VII of Norway, and, after their countries were conquered in 1941, Kings Peter of Yugoslavia and George II of Greece fled to Britain, assisting their Governments in exile in continuing the war against Hitler. In this time of occupation and defeat, they summed up in themselves their respective nations' desire to be free.

This was true also of the two who remained behind: Leopold III of Belgium and Christian X of Denmark. In the case of Leopold, he had known early on that the British intended to withdraw their troops by sea from western Belgium. As Commander in Chief of the Army, he was with his troops in the field; his government informed him that if defeated, it was necessary for King and Cabinet to continue the fight from abroad. He on the other hand believed it to be his duty to share his people's fate. On May 28, he surrendered his army, and addressed them, saying: "I will not leave you in these tragic moments. I shall stay with you to protect you and your families and your fate will be mine." The royal family were imprisoned in their palace until June 1944, when they were taken into captivity in Germany.

Because Denmark was never at war with Germany, so swift was its conquest, its king and government remained in place throughout the occupation. But every day and in defiance of German wishes, the King rode a horse through the streets of Copenhagen in Danish army uniform. To his people he carried in his own person their refusal to be other than what they were. So impressed were they by this lone and dangerous deed, that Kaj Munk, a noted Danish resistance fighter executed by the Nazis on January 4, 1944, wrote one of his most stirring poems in Christian's honor.

But for less elevated personages, things were not quite so clear. As General Weygand, who would loyally serve the Vichy regime of Marshal Petain put it: "Any man will do his duty. The tragedy comes when he must make a choice between two sign posts each marked 'duty' and pointing in opposite directions."

The first country whose inhabitants would face this question was Czechoslovakia. From the beginning, the ethnic Germans in the Sudetenland, the Slovaks, the Ruthenians, and the Magyars all faced domination by the Czechs. Among the Czechs themselves, unbelievers and Protestants (like apostate Thomas Masaryk, the nation's first President) were in power, relegating the Catholic majority, whose party led by *Fr. Jan Sramek* was dedicated to accomplishing the Church's social teachings in the country, to a minor role. The Sudeten German Party, although host to a Nazi element, was until 1938 dominated by members of the *Kameradschaftbund*, followers of Professor Othmar Spann, an Austrian Catholic conservative who was held as a dangerous enemy by the Nazis. The Ruthenians, a branch of the Ukrainians, were led in turn by *Fr. Augustin Volosin*, and the Slovak Nationalists first by *Fr. Andrej Hlinka*, and then by *Msgr. Josef Tiso*. In the beginning, the anti-clerical Czech government helped assist in the formation of a schism in 1920. That year saw a group of Catholic priests, members of a group founded in 1890 to press for things like a vernacular liturgy and the abolition of celibacy, secede to form the Czechoslovak Church. Although at first claiming to retain Catholicity, in short order its adherents abandoned the Apostolic succession, numbered the Bible as only one of many sources of revelation, held reason as the highest religious truth, declared that Christ was God's Son only ethically, rejected Original Sin; in a word, they became Unitarians. The government's support for these folk was not lost on the country's Catholics; nor were its centralizing cultural and political methods, nor were the pro-Soviet tendencies of some of its leadership, particularly after Eduard Benes became President. It seemed to many, both Czechs and those of other nationalities, that the leadership in Prague and perhaps the very State itself offered a long term threat to their religion, their culture, and perhaps (should the government become more dictatorial) their very lives.

Under these circumstances, the rise of Nazi Germany appeared to many of these people to be an opportunity for freedom. To the Sudeten Germans, and to the Magyars of southern Slovakia who were incorporated in Hungary at the same time after Munich, this seemed particularly the case. Another result of that treaty was that Benes left the country, and was replaced as President by Emil Hacha. Slovakia and Ruthenia were each given autonomous governments. When Hacha attempted to suppress Slovakia's in March of 1939, the Germans were appealed to by the Slovaks as guarantors of the Munich accords, and they very happily marched into Prague. Slovakia became independent, Ruthenia was seized by Hungary, and the rump of the Czech lands, still nominally governed by Hacha and his cabinet, became the Bohemia-Moravia Protectorate. Benes formed a Czech government in exile, while Bohemia-Moravia became an integral part of the German war efforts:

> The situation of the Czechs in the so-called Protectorate during the war was not unfavorable. In the first place they were exempt from military service, and worked quite willingly for Hitler's war machine in the Bohemian industries, which were greatly developed by the Germans. Thousands of tanks, airplanes and guns were produced in the factories, many more than could possibly have been destroyed by the Legions which were organized by Benes in France, England, and Russia. The Legion in the West, which consisted of about 5,000 men in the ground forces, never went into action, while the 12,000 men in Russia were engaged in only a few insignificant skirmishes. As Benes himself said, it was a "symbolical

army," but propaganda made quite a respectable amount
of political capital out of it, and the books and newspa-
per articles which were written about it during and after
the liberation of Prague gave the impression that the war
could scarcely have been won without its aid. However,
it would be unjust not to mention here the well-deserved
glory earned by some Czech airmen in the Battle of Britain.

Statistics show that Bohemia's war-time industrial and
agricultural production were proportionately equal to that
of Germany, and food shortages were no worse there than
in the Reich. In contrast to Poland active resistance and
sabotage scarcely existed in Bohemia until the last days
of the war, although arrests were made in Bohemia and
Moravia as in the other countries occupied by Germany,
and in Germany itself.

The assassination of Heydrich was planned and organized abroad, and the Benes government cleverly ex-
ploited the severe reprisals that followed, and especially
the shooting of the 168 male inhabitants of Lidice, to
influence British and American public opinion in its favor. Care was taken, of course, to avoid mentioning the
fact that the reprisals were not the responsibility of the
Sudeten Germans but were carried out by German Nazis
(F.O. Miksche, *Danubian Federation*, p.25).

Czechs served in large numbers in the German army,
and the Czech clergy supported Hacha because of their fear
of both the anti-clericals and the Soviets. The Czech populace as a whole was quiescent, and the result was that Prague
came through the war unscathed. It was an odd situation,
but who (save those who actually have been so in such a
spot) can claim they would have been more courageous than
the Czechs in their position?

Slovakia was a different question. Where German power

meant subordination for the Czechs, it meant independence
for the Slovaks. Msgr. Tiso and his government took the
opportunity given them to organize:

> The constitution of the Slovak Republic, adopted on
> July 31, 1939, was that of a typical parliamentary de-
> mocracy. Legislative and fiscal powers were vested in a
> one-house assembly elected by universal suffrage, which
> also chose the president of the republic and approved the
> ratification of treaties. The president conducted the gov-
> ernment with the aid of ministers responsible to the as-
> sembly and removable by vote of no confidence. The
> constitution provided for an independent judiciary and
> contained a full bill of rights and guarantees of due pro-
> cess of law. Although the government, under constant
> pressure from the Nazis, was obliged to exercise a certain
> degree of censorship, there was no violation of basic hu-
> man rights. Even the postwar Communist-dominated
> government was obliged to admit that "not a single po-
> litical execution took place in the Slovak state."

Article 79 of the Slovak Constitution grouped all citizens, regardless of social status, into "six estates"–agri-
culture, industry, commerce, banking, free professions,
and public employees–which some writers have mistak-
enly identified with the corporations of Mussolini's fascist state. These estates were not, however, copied from
Italian Fascism: they were recommended by Pope Pius
XI in his encyclical *Quadragesimo Anno*, and were self-
governing bodies in which employers and workers in each
branch of the economy could resolve their social conflicts in accord with Christian principle. Another super-
ficial resemblance to fascism lay in the para-military
Hlinka Guard, the uniforms of which looked rather like
those of Hitler's storm troopers. Here it might be commented that in borrowing some of the panoply of Fascism, Tiso and his associates hoped to distract Nazi at-

tention from the Christian orientation of the Slovak state. The Hlinka Guard conducted frequent drills, parades, and demonstrations, and helped the army and police in tasks of order and defense—it did not indulge in organized smashing of Jewish shops or liquidation of political dissenters (Kurt Glaser, *Czecho-Slovakia: A Critical History*, pp.57-58).

An American correspondent, Edward L. Delaney, who spent much of the War in Slovakia, gives a similar account in his book, *False Freedom*. But what we are to make of the Tiso regime, which, until a 1944 revolt forced him to call in German troops, pursued an independent and by and large benevolent policy? Were they traitors? To the Czechs? But again, if they were ill-advised to accept German aid, would we have known better?

The case of France is even more complex. Catholics and Monarchists had little reason to mourn the Third Republic; indeed, for such folk the defeat of France in 1940 was a divine judgment. The only way for France to return to greatness and independence was to atone for her past and shed the decadence which had caused her defeat. Thus traditionalists of all sorts (most notably Charles Maurras and the *Action Française*) rallied to Marshal Petain and the regime he headed, based at Vichy and controlling the unoccupied South of France and the colonies.

At first, their hopes seemed justified. Petain restored Catholic education to the public schools and public aid to the Catholic ones. Divorce was made much harder to get, and large families were given financial incentives. The lodges of Freemasons were closed. There was talk of restoring the provinces abolished in 1789, and subsidies given families who would reopen and operate abandoned farms. A corporatist economy was set up. No doubt many contemporaries hoped that in time a Traditional Catholic French Monarchy would rise from the ruins. But this was not to be; the Nazis had no use for that sort of thing.

As time went on Petain was forced to replace traditionalists in his government with former Socialists and even Communists like Pierre Laval, Georges Doriot, and Marcel Deat. In 1940, Petain had seemed like the incarnation of France; but the German occupation of Vichy in response to the 1942 allied seizure of North Africa and Vichy's increasing subordination to Berlin led a former pupil of Petain's to acquire the mantle: *Charles De Gaulle.*

Interestingly enough, one Monarchist who never believed that Germany meant to deal honestly with Vichy was the heir to the French throne, Henri, Comte de Paris. Having served in the French Army against the Germans under an assumed name, he left after the surrender for Morocco. There he made clear his preference for the Free French based in London under De Gaulle's headship.

De Gaulle had declared himself leader of the Free French in a British Broadcasting Corporation broadcast on June 18, 1940, in which he declared that France was undefeated; he called upon all Frenchmen desirous of continuing the war to rally to him. At the time he was a virtually unknown figure. The Marshal had been invested with authority by the last government of the Third Republic, and was recognized as Chief of the French State by all neutral powers, including the United States. At first, the entire French overseas empire rallied to Petain. De Gaulle was without any territorial base from which to carry on his fight. But in a swift series of moves, all of French Equatorial Africa rallied to him from August 26 to August 29. In those three short days, Free France acquired a home.

Flushed with victory, De Gaulle and Churchill planned an assault on the strategic Vichy held town of Dakar in Senegal. Much to their surprise, resistance was stiff, and the invaders were beaten off. This was not surprising. At this stage the Marshal's regime appeared truly independent, and De Gaulle was regarded as a traitor by perhaps the majority of Frenchmen, although in September the French possessions in the Pacific–French Oceania, French India, New Caledonia, and the New Hebrides–rallied to Free France. This notion, however, would change as the iron grip of the Nazis tightened on France. With the Communists still allied to Hitler, the early resistance within France was made up of non-Communist left-wing intellectuals and right-wing and Monarchist activists who did not trust the promises the Germans made to Petain about an armistice with honor. After the German invasion of the Soviet Union, the Communists made an about face, and in many districts came to dominate the Resistance. Thus a terrible case of divided loyalties was proffered the average Frenchman: to side with Petain, whose government was ever more under Hitler's thumb, or with De Gaulle, whose men in the field often had to collaborate with Stalin's? It was a microcosm of the European dilemma.

Whatever the case internally, more and more of the empire was slipping from Vichy's grasp. An Anglo-Free French invasion of Syria and Lebanon commenced on June 8, 1941, and concluded, after a surprisingly fierce Vichy resistance, on July 12.

America's entry into the war did not mean a severance of relations with Vichy, even though the Marshal had indicated to the American ambassador on November 18 that he was "a prisoner." Nevertheless, German seizure of strategic Vichy held colonies was a threat; nowhere was this a more severe threat than on the little French islands of St. Pierre and Miquelon off the coast of Newfoundland. It was FDR's intention to take them over using US or Canadian forces. On December 24, 1941, a small Free French flotilla seized them instead. American Secretary of State Cordell Hull sent an

insulting note to the Canadian government virtually order-
ing them to expel the Free French. The Canadians and the
British backed up De Gaulle, and the occupation of the islands was ungracefully accepted in Washington. But the natural dislike between FDR and the leader of the Free French
was cemented; Roosevelt, if he must eventually withdraw
recognition from Vichy, would find a more pliant Frenchman to run that country's war effort, if he could.

Meanwhile, the Japanese occupation of French
Indochina, Burma, Thailand, and Malaya, as well as air assaults on Ceylon, turned Allied attention to the huge French
island of Madagascar. Reasoning that Vichy's garrison would
offer little resistance to the Japanese, it was decided by
Churchill that the island must be taken. But knowing that
FDR would be upset at any participation by De Gaulle, he
ordered that it would be a purely British operation. On May
6, 1942 the assault began. At that time the US State Department announced that Madagascar would be returned to
France after the war. Incensed, De Gaulle demanded satisfaction from Churchill. The result was that a week later the
British Foreign Office announced that once the country was
secured it would be turned over to Free French administration.

In July of 1942, it was agreed by the British and Americans that, preparatory to landings on the continent of Europe, French North Africa as well as Libya had to be taken
by the Allies. It was also agreed that the Free French were to
have no part in it, despite their valor in Libya, where their
troops had won a great victory at Bir Hacheim against
Rommels' Afrika Korps. Operation Torch, as it was to be
called, was to be bloodless. To accomplish this goal, Roosevelt
would have to find his replacement for De Gaulle:

Roosevelt's objective was to find a Frenchman who, by lending his name to Torch, would give to an act of aggression the appearance of an act of liberation. He recognized that Vichy might order its forces in North Africa to resist the landings. A Frenchman of great stature, he believed, could persuade the troops that it was in the interest of France to lay down its arms. Roosevelt set out, even before Torch had been decided, to find a Frenchman who could unite all Frenchmen under United States leadership (Milton Viorst, *Hostile Allies: FDR and De Gaulle*, p.97).

There it was in a nutshell. What the New Deal had been to America in terms of subjecting every facet of life to government control, so would American participation in the War be. Independent allies (save, as we shall see, the Soviet Union) could not be tolerated. The British Empire through her economic and military dependence upon us and the cession of her bases even before the War had already been reduced to a junior partner. The same should happen to France. For all his failings, De Gaulle was resolved that this would not happen to his country.

General Maxime Weygand, an independent minded old soldier whose German-ordered dismissal from the Vichy cabinet was the occasion of Petain's declaration to the American ambassador earlier cited, was approached and offered the role of leader after the invasion. He angrily refused, and informed the Marshal of Allied plans. The US then turned to General Henri Giraud, who had recently escaped from a German prison and pledged his allegiance to Petain at Vichy.

On November 8, 1942, Operation Torch began. Three days earlier, Giraud had arrived in Algiers, to be ready to take control as civil administrator of North Africa when the invasion was over. De Gaulle broadcast over the B.B.C. an appeal to the French in North Africa to rise up and join the Allies.

Petain, in the meantime, who had warned the Americans after Weygand told him of the plot that he would resist any invasion, gave the following reply to the American ambassador who presented a conciliatory note from FDR:

> It is with stupor and with grief that I learned during the night of the aggression of your troops against North Africa.
>
> I have read your message. You invoke pretexts which nothing justifies. You attribute to your enemies intentions which have never been manifested in acts. I have always declared that we would defend our empire if it were attacked. You knew that we would defend it against any aggressor whoever he might be. You knew that I would keep my word.
>
> In our misfortune I had, when requesting the Armistice, protected our Empire and it is you who, acting in the name of a country to which so many memories and ties bind us, have taken such a cruel initiative.
>
> France and her honor are at stake.
> We are attacked.
> We shall defend ourselves.
> This is the order I am giving.

To Petain, the assaults on Algiers, Oran, and Casablanca appeared to be cut from the same cloth as Pearl Harbor.

Meanwhile, Admiral Darlan, commander in chief in North Africa, and formerly Petain's premier (until replaced at German insistence with ex-Socialist Laval) called for a cease fire two days later, while wondering what next to do; the Germans saved him the trouble of further thought by occupying the unoccupied zone of France the next day.

Darlan assumed complete civil control of French North

Africa, and accepted Giraud as military commander. The Germans occupied Tunisia with Italian aid, but the French troops in eastern Algeria, now united with the Allies, kept them from advancing further west. Darlan still professed to be subject to the Marshal, with American approval. De Gaulle was obviously to be cut out.

Nevertheless, as 1942 drew to a close, a certain impasse was reached: three factions behind Darlan, Giraud, and De Gaulle kept a sort of uneasy logroll between them. On December 24th, Darlan was assassinated by a young Monarchist army officer, Bonnier de la Chapelle. It was his hope that this would precipitate a coup in favor of the Count of Paris, who was in Algiers (ironically, after having returned from trying to persuade Petain to allow the Allies to seize North Africa peacefully). Indeed, there was much support for such a move. The chief of police, Henri d'Astier, was plotting such a coup, but was quickly arrested.

On Christmas Day, General Eisenhower arrived in Algiers. At his behest the French authorities in Algiers made Giraud Darlan's successor. Friction between De Gaulle and Giraud—and so between Churchill and Roosevelt—festered.

But Algeria was not everything. In late November, 1942, the Indian Ocean island of Reunion passed from Vichy hands to De Gaulle. At the same time, half the officers, two thirds of the non-commissioned officers, and all of the men of the Madagascar garrison, after surrendering to the British, joined the Free French. The remainder volunteered for service with Giraud. The next month, French Somaliland with its 8,000 troops joined De Gaulle. General Leclerc led his troops from Chad through the Libyan desert and linked up with Montgomery. Every such victory eroded Giraud's position further.

Most ironic was the fact that, despite acting in great part for Roosevelt, Giraud was committed to the principles of

Vichy. In order to justify American support, Giraud had to make a profession of belief in liberal democracy on March 14, 1943. Without bringing him republican support, it lost him his Vichy allies in North Africa. From this point on, he represented only FDR. Rewarding him, the US prevented de Gaulle's representative from taking over in French Guiana when the Vichy administration there was overthrown. Interning him in Trinidad, they flew in one of Giraud's men instead.

When, in early May, Tunis at last fell, both de Gaulle's men and Giraud's were present at the victory. But afterwards, many of the latter went over to the Free French, inspired as much by Leclerc's epic march across the desert as anything else. On May 15th, De Gaulle received from his liaison with the Resistance in France their acceptance of his leadership. Later that month, Giraud gave in and acknowledged De Gaulle as head of fighting France. Roosevelt was foiled; France had an Allied government which was now in charge of the French Colonial Empire and insisted upon being treated as an equal partner with the US, the British Empire, and the Soviet Union.

A number of our allies were not so fortunate. As with Czechoslovakia, Yugoslavia was a creation of Versailles and Woodrow Wilson, and included a number of irreconcilable elements. Serbia had, before 1914, acquired Macedonia, the largest number of whose people were ethnically connected to the Bulgarians. In the region of Kossovo were many Albanians who looked over the border to their independent nation, wrapped in chaos as it was. To this primarily Eastern Orthodox country were added in 1918 Bosnia-Hercegovina (primarily Moslem with Orthodox Serb and Catholic Croat minorities), and Catholic Croatia and Slovenia, as well as ethnically Serb but fiercely independent Montenegro. Over this gimcrack collection of peoples reigned first Prince Regent and then (after the death of his father Peter I) King Alexander. The King desired a centralized state under Serbian control; the Slovenes and Croats wanted a federation. *Fr. Anton Korosec* (1872-1940) was a Jesuit and leader of the Slovene people, who like the Slovaks looked traditionally to the Catholic clergy for leadership.

In Croatia, however, secular nationalist thought had long had a strong presence, as in Poland. Croats and Serbs clashed repeatedly on the political front, making parliamentary government very difficult. The assassination of the Prime Minister in 1928 led King Alexander to take direct control of the country. Rather than reigning as monarch of all his peoples, it became his policy to "Serbianize" the nation, outlawing Croatian and Slovene national symbols and using exclusively Serb ones. The Croatian opposition as well as the Communists were keenly persecuted by the regime. In 1932, the Croatian nationalists united to oppose the royal government. Numbers of them were murdered by the secret police, and they retaliated in kind. At last, on October 9, 1934, King Alexander was assassinated in Marseilles by Croat nationalists.

Since Alexander's son, Peter II, was a boy of 11 years when his father died, a regency was established, under the King's cousin, Prince Paul. Under the Regent, Yugoslavia returned to parliamentary rule with its attendant division and low scale chaos. The Croatian Nationalist Movement, the Ustasha, continued its conflict with the government.

In the meantime, war broke out, and France fell in June of 1940. This put Romania and Yugoslavia, traditional French allies, in a very bad position; due to the Soviet-German pact, the two powers most desirous of gobbling up the Balkans were allied. Romania in particular was in a bad position. King Carol II, a noted immoralist and indifferent politician, had established a nominally corporatist state under his own control in 1938. During this time the Iron Guard, despite initial persecution by Carol (resulting in the death of founder *Corneliu Codreanu)* gathered enough strength that the King was forced to appoint Guard sympathizer General Ion Antonescu to the Defense Ministry. After the fall of France, Carol was forced by Germany and the Soviet Union to cede Bessarabia to the Soviets, half of Transylvania to Hungary, and Southern Dobrudja to Bulgaria. So great was the outcry that on September 18, Carol made Antonescu Prime Minister, and two days later abdicated. His 19-year-old son Michael became King, but real power was in the hands of Antonescu. Despite appearances, the now-Marshal Antonescu was so subservient to the Germans that the next year he ordered a bloody purge of the Iron Guard, who demonstrated that their primary loyalty was to Romania and not Germany. In short order, Romania, Bulgaria, Hungary, and Slovakia joined the Rome-Berlin-Tokyo Axis.

Now Yugoslavia's position was tenuous indeed. With Italian-controlled Albania in its rear, and the Italian, German, Hungarian, Romanian, and Bulgarian frontiers all occupied by Axis troops, Prince Paul was easily convinced that his nation's survival lay with the Germans. On March 25, 1941, he signed an agreement bringing his nation into the Axis. This precipitated a coup by Serbian Nationalist Army officers, who resented the Regent's recent accord with Croatian leaders. They denounced the pact with the Axis.

German reaction was swift: on April 6 German, Italian, Hungarian and Bulgarian troops surged across the border; totally outflanked, the Yugoslav army capitulated on April 17. King Peter and his government fled to London, and the country was partitioned. Macedonia was given to Bulgaria, half of Banat and another small district to Hungary, Dalmatia, Kossovo, and half of Slovenia to Italy, and the remaining Slovene portion to Germany herself. Montenegro was placed under Italian occupation, and the rump of Serbia, run by former Minister of War General Nedic, under German. Croatia was declared an independent state under Ustasha leader Ante Pavelic, who then declared the country a monarchy and the Italian Duke of Spoleto (cousin of the Italian King) was given the throne under the title Tomislav I. He never entered his putative realm, however.

The new Croatian state immediately began to settle old scores with the Serbs–these old scores became the murder of some 250,000 Serbs, an act condemned by Cardinal Stepinac, Archbishop of Zagreb, as well as by the dean of Croatian nationalists, Vladimir Macek. The latter for his pains spent the war years in jail. But it should be pointed out that many sincere Croats joined the Ustasha simply because it promised a national renaissance.

Resistance to the Germans broke out in their zone of Serbia under Colonel Draza Mihailovic. A staunch Royalist and Serb nationalist, Mihailovic organized his guerrillas under the name of "Chetniks," the name used by similar bands who had fought the Turks centuries before. They soon scored many successes against the invaders. It should be noted, however, that while Draza Mihailovic was preferable to the communist Tito, relatively speaking, he was a Serb bigot who promoted the idea of "ethnic cleansing."

The Communists, in the meantime, began hostilities after the invasion of the Soviet Union, calling themselves Partisans. Led by Josip Broz (Tito) they soon became the rivals of the Chetniks, who had been recognized by King Peter II as his representatives. But Churchill and Roosevelt came to favor Tito, as did of course, their ally Stalin. Having prevented an attempt by Peter to parachute in and join his men, the Allies in 1943 switched their allegiance from Mihailovich to Tito, and forced Peter to recognize him. When the Italians surrendered in 1943, they were instructed to surrender their arms and territory to the Partisans, thus placing Tito's men in a position to control the country in 1944, when the Germans at last withdrew.

Albania underwent a similar travail. There too, after an initial outbreak by royalist resistance loyal to the exiled King Zog I, the German invasion brought forth Communist guerrillas led by one Enver Hoxha. In time, they alone received Western aid, thus ensuring Hoxha's control when the Germans pulled out.

In all the Balkans, only Greece managed to escape Communism's maw and regain its King; this was due to Churchill's actions in the teeth of Roosevelt's opposition. Part of the reason was that Greece's George II was the close cousin of Britain's George VI; added to this was the fact that, as in Albania and Yugoslavia, the only alternative to Communism in Greece was in fact the King. Greece's strategic situation vis-à-vis the Suez Canal had brought British troops when the Germans invaded at the same time as they attacked Yugoslavia. Swiftly conquering the mainland, the Germans at last took the last Anglo-Greek refuge in Crete. The royal family fled to South Africa, where they got to know the country's Prime Minister, Jan Smuts, very well. They then proceeded to London for the duration.

Greece lost Macedonia to Bulgaria and the Ionian islands to Italy. The remainder of the country was under German occupation, nominally under the control of a Greek general who defected to the Axis. As in the rest of the Balkans, Communist guerrillas used the War to extend their control over the countryside. Unlike the rest of the Balkans, when the Germans withdrew in October 1944, British troops arrived to replace them. The Greek government returned to Athens, but opposition to the King's return on the part of the Allied leadership, despite the pleas of General Alexandros Papagos who led the Greek Army against the Communists, remained.

Poland, whose territorial integrity was, after all, the alleged reason for the war, faced a similar dilemma. Unlike the other occupied nations, in Poland there was no collaboration; the Poles were all too aware that Nazi racial theory had slated their nobility, priesthood, and intelligentsia for destruction, and the remainder of the populace to serfdom. A proud Catholic people, the Poles did not submit easily, either to their German or their Soviet invaders.

Almost immediately after the defeat of the Polish Army and the establishment of the government-in-exile in London, the Polish underground organized as the Polish Home Army. It functioned in fact as a clandestine Polish government. After the invasion of the Soviet Union by Germany, the invaders discovered the barbarous murder of Polish officers by the Soviets at the Katyn Forest. Yet these were the folk with whom first Churchill and then FDR directed the Poles to cooperate!

Polish insistence on an inquiry into the Katyn murders led to a rupture between their governments in London and Moscow. The Soviets created their own Polish Communist government, to which the few Communist guerrillas and the Poles fighting in the Soviet Army gave their allegiance. But the Polish Home Army, under its heroic "General Bor" (actually Taddeusz Count Komorowsky) spread throughout the country and gathered ever more strength. When the Soviets had advanced as far as the suburbs of Warsaw, they encouraged the Home Army to rise and take Warsaw, which was done on August 1, 1944. Rather than advance to their aid, however, the Soviets sat calmly by while the Germans besieged the city, eventually reconquering it on October 2. The fighting had destroyed the Home Army, at the time of the Warsaw Rising a powerful armed force which could have served to defend Poland from the Soviets after the War; it also exhausted the Germans, so that in a mere two months after the surrender of General Bor, the Soviets moved into the devastated city.

The War on the Eastern Front typified the reasons for the Nazis' eventual defeat. On June 22, 1941, just before dawn, Germany attacked the Soviet Union. All along the front, from Finland to the Black Sea, the Wehrmacht advanced. Finland, which had lost an unequal conflict (and much territory) to the Soviets in 1939-40, joined the Germans; with them too were Italian, Hungarian, Romanian, and Slovakian troops. Eventually, although Franco refused to enter the War, Spanish volunteers arrived. On that June day the entire nature of the struggle changed. All over the world, the Communist parties switched sides: from acting as informants for the Germans against the resistance in occupied countries, they became "patriots"; in the US, they abandoned isolationism and insisted on American entry into the conflict. Stalin felt personally betrayed, since Hitler he had always regarded as a kindred spirit.

At first, the advance was easy going, indeed. The Red Army, devastated by purges in 1936, was no match for the invaders. Moreover, since the German government's rhetoric about Communism was taken at face value (even as Petain and other "collaborators" had taken its talk about European unity) the advancing troops, after the initial battles were over, found themselves greeted in many towns and villages by children with flowers. Had the Nazi racial theory not interfered, the War in the East could have been won.

But it did so interfere. When General von Leeb, Commander of the Northern Group of German Armies, had surrounded Leningrad, he was in a position to march right into the city. He was stopped by Hitler's personal order:

> Years later in Washington [German General] von Boetticher told [American General Albert Wedermeyer]

that Hitler wanted von Leeb to continue his siege of the city so that its two million inhabitants would slowly starve. This tied down important elements of von Leeb's forces. Eventually von Leeb's reserves were taken away and moved to hard-pressed southern areas with the result that he no longer had sufficient forces to capture Leningrad. Thus Hitler's demographic sadism kept von Leeb from delivering a decisive blow to Russian resistance. Today the Communists celebrate justifiably the heroic defense of Leningrad, but it was probably the intercession of Hitler that prevented professional German military leaders from taking the city (Albert C. Wedemeyer, *Wedemeyer Reports!*, p.415).

In matters of tactics and strategy, Hitler interfered; but also in matters of internal administration. The familiar apparatus of oppression was imported, and a marvelous chance to truly unite the peoples of the East lost. Instead of Latvia, Lithuania, and Estonia being freed, they were lumped with Byelorussia in the Reichskomissariat of Ostland; the Ukraine was similarly constituted a Reichskomissariat. Alfred Rosenberg, chief racial theorist of the Nazi Party was placed in charge of these two areas; he was to supervise Germanization of the regions and the rounding up of slave-workers for the Reich industrial machine. In his *Myth of the Twentieth Century*, he had set forward the party's racial theory. Most interesting for our point of view was Rosenberg's opinion of Catholicism:

Rosenberg denounced Christianity as a dangerous product of the Semitic-Latin spirit and a disintegrative Judaistic concept. Christian churches, he wrote, especially the Roman Catholic Church, are "prodigious, conscious, and unconscious falsifications." The Old Testament should be abandoned as a book of religion, because it was responsible for "our present Jewish domination." For the Old Testament cattle breeders Rosenberg would substitute the Nordic sagas and fairy tales. Instead of what he called the murdering messiahship he would have "the dream of honor and freedom rekindled by the Nordic, Germanic sagas." The true picture of Christ, he asserted, had been distorted by Jewish fanatics like Matthew, by materialistic rabbis like Paul, by African jurists like Tertullian, and by mongrel half-breeds like St. Augustine. The real Christ, Rosenberg insisted, was an Amorite Nordic, aggressive and courageous, a revolutionary who opposed the Jewish and Roman systems with sword in hand, bringing not peace but war. Popes and Jesuits, in Rosenberg's view, had made Christianity unrecognizable, and the heroic Luther and Calvin had been frustrated by their followers.

Rosenberg reserved his utmost contempt for the Roman Catholic Church. It had kept civilization in slavery, and it remained a pitiless force working against the Nordic ideal. Roman Catholicism, he wrote, was an even greater menace than Judaism because its roots were tenacious in history. It had made the fundamental error of taking into its fold any human being regardless of his racial origin—a crime against the ideal of racial purity. The Catholic doctrines of love and pity were directly contrary to the Germanic virtues of heroism and honor. There were irreconcilable differences between the Catholic and Christian mentalities. Catholicism sprang from Oriental races in Judaea and Syria and was therefore alien to the spirit of Nordicism. Spiritually, the Catholic clergy was a continuation of the old Etruscan priesthood. The Pope was merely a medicine man, and Church history only a series of atrocities, forgeries, and swindles.

As a Nazi ideologist, Rosenberg demanded that the "white race" be freed from the disruptive Etruscan-Syrio-Judaic-Asiatic-Catholic influence. This influence was, he charged, a monstrous perversion of truth. The German people must turn away from the medicine man Pope and his voodoo practices, from mongrelized Catholicism, from the Old Testament, from the decadent morals of the Sermon on the Mount, and from the doctrine of sin and salvation. These should be replaced by the swastika as the living symbol of race and blood (Dr. Louis L. Snyder, *Encyclopedia of the Third Reich*, p.301).

This was the chap who would determine policies in the two Reichskommissariaten. Polish Galicia was given over to the Government General, that body which administered the rump of Poland not directly annexed to Germany. Romania was allowed to reoccupy the territory the Soviets had taken, and a bit more besides. Outside of the Romanian zone, however, German treatment of the civilian population led directly to the formation of partisan groups directed from Moscow.

Despite such ill-treatment, however, thousands of Cossacks, Ukrainians, Kalmucks, Tartars, Lithuanians, Latvians, Estonians, Byelorussians, Armenians, Georgians, and Turkestanis, were recruited into the German military. Moreover, a million Russians were recruited, most of whom were ultimately commanded by General Vlassov, an ex-Soviet General. The poor usage of his men—and that of the anti-Communist eastern volunteers as a whole—was seen only too well by the German liaison, Colonel Claus Count von Stauffenberg. A pious Catholic and hater of both Bolshevism and National Socialism, Stauffenberg saw in Hitler's and the Nazi machine's treatment of the East, Germany's doom.

So it would prove. The resistance which Stalin was able to mount, reinforced by America after Pearl Harbor, tied up enormous amounts of Axis men and materiel. In 1943, the Allies crossed over into Sicily; that island seized, they attacked the mainland of Italy itself. At last, the Allies having taken Naples, on July 25, King Victor Emmanuel III dismissed and ordered imprisoned Mussolini. The King's own description of the event is worth quoting:

> This morning [July 25th, 1943] Mussolini asked me for an interview which I fixed for this afternoon at 4:00pm at this villa. When he arrived Mussolini told me that a meeting of the Fascist Grand Council had been held and had passed a vote of censure on him, but he believed that this resolution was not in order. I replied at once that I did not agree with him; the Grand Council was an organ of state which he himself had created by means of a law which had been passed by the Chamber and Senate; therefore every decision of the Grand Council was valid. "Then according to Your Majesty I ought to resign," he said with considerable violence. "Yes," I answered, and told him that I forthwith accepted his resignation.

He appointed Marshal Pietro Badoglio as Prime Minister. Hitler struck fast; German troops seized all territory not held by the Allies, despite a spirited resistance by Italian soldiers. The King and his government were forced to flee to Bari in the South. Mussolini was sprung from jail in a daring raid, and given headship of the Italian Social Republic (which consisted of all Italian soil occupied by the Germans). Yard by bloody yard the Allies (now including the Kingdom of Italy) pushed the Germans up the Italian peninsula.

At about the same time, the wily King Boris III of Bulgaria died shortly after a visit to Hitler. He had sheltered Gypsies, Jews, and other folk the Nazis wanted; had refused to send troops to Russia; and in all things preserved as independent a policy as he could. His mysterious death has been ascribed to both Nazis and Communists, both of whom stood to gain. His six-year-old son, Simeon II, succeeded him under a regency led by Boris's brother, Prince Cyril. The boy-King's mother, Queen Giovanna, was the daughter of Victor Emmanuel, and feared that, after her father changed sides, they would be menaced. Sure enough, Hitler demanded to be made Simeon's guardian. The Queen Mother smuggled herself and her royal child out of the country to Turkey.

The Eastern Front continued to deteriorate, and in June, 1944, D-Day opened a third front in France. It was obvious that Germany was about to be defeated. Thus it was that on July 20, 1944, the famous Stauffenberg coup was attempted against Hitler.

The German Resistance was a varied one. From the beginning, however, it was in particular dominated by Army officers, nobles, Catholic and Protestant churchmen, and the like. Its greatest organizer was Karl Goerdeler, sometime Lord Mayor of Leipzig, and its theorists Helmuth von Moltke and the diverse members of the "Kreisau" (his county estate) circle. The ideology of the most active members of the Resistance is very enlightening:

> An examination of the ideas and programs of the leading conspirators against Hitler reveals the existence of two concerns: limitations on political participation by the masses, and moral reconstruction of the "mass man." Naturally, the ideas of the Resistance were in no sense identical with all the grotesque variations of the anti-Weimar ideology. Above all, the conspirators had in good measure broken with nationalism, which had been the basis and the cement of the Conservative Revolution [the Right-Wing opposition to Weimar]. Nevertheless, both major concerns of the Resistance were derived from the Conservative Revolution. Moreover, despite the presence of a few persons of old-fashioned liberal persuasions, and of a few Socialists, the anti-Nazi Resistance was borne by heirs of the conservative anti-Weimar movement. Their attitudes and interests determined the flow of events in the conspiracy. Their ideas–thoroughly reminiscent of the tone and content of Conservative longings during the Weimar period, though now increasingly betraying a

turn from the realm of politics to the realm of religious
and moral transformation–molded the programs for the
future (George K. Romoser, "The Politics of Uncertainty:
The German Resistance Movement," in Hans-Adolf
Jacobsen, ed., *July 20, 1944: Germans Against Hitler*,
pp.72-73).

Time after time, the Resistance plotted either coups or
assassination attempts against Hitler. The first named collapsed time after time because the contemplated Allied victory–over the Rhineland, Czechoslovakia, or wherever, never
materialized. When FDR entered the War, and made it clear
that unconditional surrender was all that would be acceptable to him, the chances of the Resistance were reduced even
further: they could not offer prospective supporters even the
assurance that Hitler's overthrow would result in a negotiated peace.

But as the situation became ever more desperate, it was
realized that desperate measures would have to be taken. A
figure arose willing to what must be done to do away with
Hitler and inaugurate a new regime: Colonel Claus Count
von Stauffenberg, whom we met in Russia. Wounded (los-
ing a leg, part of a hand, and an eye) in North Africa,
Stauffenberg believed that God had preserved him purely to
rescue his Fatherland. Handsome, stalwart, a good father and
husband, von Stauffenberg was truly a figure of chivalry. As
co-conspirator Axel Baron von dem Bussche recalled three
years later: "Only under three assumptions can Claus
Stauffenberg be understood: his origin from a family of
Swabian knights, his Catholic upbringing, and his own intellectual world in the environment of Stefan George, with
whom he was closely associated."

Had the coup succeeded, the new government, headed
by General Ludwig Beck as Regent (a new Kaiser–probably
Louis Ferdinand–would be established afterwards) would

have looked for a negotiated peace in the West, and a successful completion of the War in the East. It was the stated desire of the plotters to "establish a state in accordance with the Christian traditions of the Western world, and based upon the principles of civic duty, loyalty, service, and achievement for the common good as well as on respect for the individual and his natural rights as a human being" (Fabian von Schlabrendorff, *The Secret War against Hitler*, p.213). The new government would press for a united Christian Europe.

The plan was for von Stauffenberg to leave a bomb next to Hitler in his East Prussian headquarters, then quickly return to Berlin and direct a coup against the surviving Nazi personnel in the capital from the Army Headquarters on the Bendlerstrasse. In the event, Hitler was not killed, the coup collapsed, and von Stauffenberg and three others were shot in the courtyard of the Bendlerstrasse building. In the months that followed, some 2,000 people were judicially murdered in connection with the plot.

Today, the building where the four men died is located on the now-named Stauffenbergerstrasse. In the courtyard is a memorial in the form of a naked man manacled. On its pedestal are the words:

> YOU DID NOT TOLERATE SHAME,
> YOU DEFENDED YOURSELVES AGAINST IT,
> YOU GAVE THE GREAT AND WATCHFUL
> SIGNAL FOR THE CHANGE,
> SACRIFICING YOUR ARDENT LIFE
> FOR LIBERTY, JUSTICE, AND HONOR

The Nazi Party became ever more tight-handed in the diminishing territories left them. In the West, almost all of France was cleared of German troops, and the Allies took Belgium and began to push into Germany. Although the Battle of the Bulge signified a short lived exercise of German strength, no one believed now that they would win. In September, the Soviets arrived at the Romanian border; the 23-year-old King Michael overthrew Antonescu in a daring maneuver at great personal risk, and the new government joined the allies, as did the Regency in Bulgaria. October saw the German withdrawal from Greece, Albania, and Yugoslavia. The next month, Hungary's Admiral Horthy attempted to pull his nation out of the Axis; he was overthrown by the Germans, who occupied the nation until the Soviets rolled over it. Relentlessly, the Italian, Western, and Eastern fronts pushed toward one another until the Third Reich was a bunch of scattered pockets.

The Battle of Berlin ended in April 1945; when it was over, Hitler was dead, and the city shattered; the "thousand year Reich" would survive its Führer by mere days. On May 8, 1945, the War in Europe ended. The Nazi regime, which had claimed the lives of such as St. Maximilian Kolbe, Bl. Titus Brandsma, Bl. Rupert Mayer, and Bl. Benedicta of the Cross, as well as innumerable other priests, religious, and lay folk (to say nothing of the many Gypsies, Jews, and others who were done to death), was over. In their reign over Europe, the Nazis had raised and dashed the hopes of numerous nationalities, from the Bretons to the Ukrainians, for independence. Those who longed for a restoration of Christian Europe either cooperated with the Axis and were destroyed or discredited by their association with them, or else joined the resistance and found themselves either destroyed by Communist colleagues or co-opted by Social Democratic ones. Hitler, Roosevelt, and Stalin shared a disdain for Catholic claims, for monarchy and nobility, for all that Old Europe had been, however much their "positive programs" may have differed. For all that Hitler hated the fate of the Nazi Party in 1945, he could not have been too upset by the downfall of altar and throne. For the first time since the year 800, the Holy See was completely without temporal allies (save Spain and Portugal).

The War in Asia had followed a somewhat similar course, in that there were the same factors of collaboration and resistance, of nationalism and dominance, as in Europe. To reign alongside Pu-Yi in Manchukuo, the heroic Mongol Prince Teh was given headship of Inner Mongolia under the Japanese; former left-wing Kuomintang man and colleague of Chiang Kai Shek, Wang Ching Wei, was given nominal headship of those sections of China under Japanese occupation. Because these men led regimes whose primary rhetorical focus was opposition to Chinese and Soviet Communism, they are dismissed as mere collaborators.

Thailand was the only pre-existing independent nation to ally with Japan, and so received portions of Laos and Cambodia in return. After Pearl Harbor, Japanese forces steadily unseated the Europeans and Americans from their territories: French Indo-China, the Philippines, the Dutch East Indies, and British-held Burma, and Malaya. On February 14, 1943, the British General Perceval surrendered the last bastion at Singapore. The losses to the British Empire numbered in excess of 166,600 men.

In their conquered territories, the Japanese installed various nationalist leaders to preside over allied governments: Jose Laurel in the Philippines, Ba Maw in Burma, Sukarno in Indonesia, and so on. These would change sides at the last minute, and claim recognition from the Allies as co-combatants. The Communists among their adherents—and among the anti-Japanese resistance—grew in strength and position, in hopes that after the War they might dictate the peace. In China the Reds under Mao Tse Tung used the War to consolidate their gains in the countryside, so that they would be able to commence again their fight against the Nationalist government afterwards.

While the Allies valiantly fought their way back through island chains, Burma, and so on, and although such battles as Iwo Jima and Okinawa are tributes to the valor of the American fighting man, the War against Japan (as against Germany) was waged very much through bombing. Just as the Germans launched the Blitz against targets in Britain, so too did the Americans and British carpet bomb Germany; such cities as Hamburg, Berlin, and especially Dresden were hard hit. Over ten times the number of German as British civilians died as a result of bombing raids. The Allies made a specialty of what was called "Baedeker Bombing"; selecting targets particularly for their cultural or historic rather than military value.

Much the same occurred in Japan, culminating in the dropping of the newly-invented atom bomb. Hiroshima felt the first one on August 6, 1945, while Nagasaki received one three days later. James Bryant Conant, President of Harvard and inventor of poison gas employed by the AEF in World War I, declared that the Japanese were subhuman and ought to have six more dropped on them. The Japanese Empire, at the insistence of Emperor Hirohito, surrendered on August 14. The greatest conflagration mankind had known since the Great Flood was over.

What sort of world would result? This had been a matter of great contention throughout the War. For Stalin and his minions, the answer was obvious: Communists the world over worked to make the globe one Soviet Republic. FDR had his own ideas, which his successor, Harry Truman, attempted to put into practice after Roosevelt's death on April 12, 1945.

There had been a number of conferences between Churchill, Stalin, and Roosevelt. That at Teheran had mostly to do with the conduct of the War and refusal to deal with any German government save on terms of unconditional surrender. At Yalta, the Soviets were promised suzerainty over Eastern Europe, and, in return for their entry into the War against Japan (with whom they were not then belligerents) control of Manchuria. The result of this latter was their establishment of a safe haven for the Chinese Reds after the War, as well as their equipping them with captured Japanese weapons. As a final note, Stalin was promised that all Soviet born prisoners taken from Axis forces would be turned over to the Red Army; thus was born the infamous "Operation Keel Haul," in which thousands of men, women, and children were turned over to their enemies. All were slaughtered, often in the hearing of the American or British troops who turned them over. With Truman replacing FDR, the three confederates met again at Potsdam after the War ended, and finalized such things as the occupation zones of Germany, Austria, and Korea.

THE COLD WAR BEGINS

The Communists immediately began reorganizing their conquests. In Yugoslavia, Bulgaria, Albania, and Hungary, rigged plebiscites abolished the Monarchy. Romania's King Michael with his sterling record of anti-Axis activity held on until the last day of 1947, when he too was at last driven out. In those countries and in Poland, Czechoslovakia, and Eastern Germany, the pattern was for the most part the same. The industrialists and landowners would lose their properties and often their lives. Coalition governments dominated by Communists would become ever more restrictive, abolishing freedom of speech and the press. The Church would be persecuted, and many of its most active people driven underground. A secret police would ferret out and destroy opposition to the regime. By handing Eastern Europe over to Stalin, we played our part in this horror which has only recently lifted.

In China, we refused to arm Chiang Kai Shek as we had promised; this was fine payment for his three times refusing a separate peace with Japan, which would have freed his nation at the price of unleashing 1,000,000 men of the Japanese Kwangtung Army against the West Coast. After a particularly bloody Civil War, the Nationalists were driven from the mainland to the large island of Taiwan in 1949. The year before, Churchill (defeated by Labour candidate Clement Attlee in 1945) had made his famous speech regarding the new order of things in Europe: "From Stettin, in the Baltic, to Trieste, on the Adriatic, an Iron Curtain has descended across the Continent." That phrase, "Iron Curtain" came to be universally known as the border between Communism and the rest of Europe.

But just what was the rest of Europe and the world to be like? It would be a grave mistake to think that the ruling circles in Britain and America were far different in their vision, ultimately, from the Soviets. Proof of this comes from what was done in those sections of Europe under their sway. The Communists executed thousands of Frenchmen and women as collaborators, with Allied tolerance; most of these, in the event, were not German sympathizers but simply the same sorts of folk eliminated by the Communists in countries where Soviet armies gave complete control to them. When order was restored under De Gaulle, this activity ceased. Similarly, the Communists of Belgium made it clear that if Leopold III returned as King to Belgium, they would make the country ungovernable. To preserve peace, Leopold abdicated in favor of his son, Baudouin.

But on a less bloody note, the war against traditional institutions, beliefs, and practices was as great in the West as in the East. The experience of Greece shows this. When Greece was liberated in October 1944, its King wished to return; this was blocked by the Allies, and it in fact took a plebiscite after the War to reinstate him. George Heaton Nicholls, wartime High Commissioner to Great Britain from South Africa (where, as we saw, the Greek Royal Family had spent time and made the acquaintance of Prime Minister Jan Smuts), commented upon this in his memoirs:

> When I arrived in London, the King of Hellenes had a suite of rooms at Claridge's and on occasions I was the bearer of messages between the King and Smuts. As the channel through which these communications passed, I found myself in a most peculiar and somewhat embarrassing position. The King was striving hard to induce the British government to allow him to return to Athens where he felt his presence on the spot, as the constitutional head of the country, would overcome much of the hostility in the political field and would rally the Greek people as a whole to defence of the constitution.
>
> On the other hand, Churchill, as head of the National Government, found himself placed with many who believed that any support given to the King of Greece would damage the reputation of the British Government. Thus it was that Churchill was being pushed to overthrow the King and support the mob law which called itself democracy. The King of Greece told me that he had been talked to like a hireling by Churchill on this subject.
>
> The policy of the British Government was, therefore, to restrain the King and I found myself the bearer of messages from Smuts to him which I knew were in direct conflict with the policy of the British Government. Once, when I pointed out to the General the compromising position I was in, he said: "Give my message to the King. The British Government is aware of my attitude." The result of the plebiscite which later voted over-

whelmingly for in favor of the return of the King, showed
that Smuts' prescience throughout was correct.

The opposition to the return of the King existed just
as strongly in the United States, Australia, and New
Zealand, as it did in some political circles in the United
Kingdom. The outcome of the plebiscite betrayed the
failure of all these people to understand the deep spiritual significance and mysticism which surrounds a hereditary ruler fulfilling his predestined task and how cu-
riously unaware they were of the loyalty for a crowned
head which exists among all common peoples who have
not been influenced by revolutionary propaganda. Those
of us who have had experience in the administration of
native tribes in Africa, know with what a deep sense of
satisfaction an hereditary chief is accepted as their spokes-
man to the world. Centuries of tradition and ritual are
not easily erased by the arguments of the London School
of Economics, however logical these may be (*South Africa in My Time*, pp.372-373).

So it was in Italy. Robert Gayre, who served as a sort of
Minister of Education for the Allied Military Government
of Italy after the deposition of Mussolini in 1943 wrote
graphically of the attitudes of his American colleagues in
that regime: "We are well aware of the attitude of vast sections of the American people to the war. It was not to restore
Poland from German aggression solely. They had dreamed
up for themselves a mission of removing 'oppression' everywhere, putting the underdog on top and pulling down 'privilege'—and bringing the blessings of American 'civilization' to
the 'barbarians,' beyond their own frontiers. The intense
nationalism of many of the Americans easily allowed such
an atmosphere to develop" (*A Case for Monarchy*, p.41). In a
note on the same page, Gayre goes on to say:

In pursuance of this self-appointed role of the "Great

Republic of the West," I was solemnly assured by some Americans that it was not necessary for me to retain the teaching of Latin and religion in the school text-books of Italy–and that what Italy needed was the introduction of a technological civilization such as existed in America– of which jeeps, refrigerators, and mass production gen- erally were the outward and evident tokens. When one remonstrated, and talked of European culture, of the part that Italy had played in the Renaissance, the need to re- tain cultural subjects in an age becoming all too rapidly mechanized, and the importance of religious instruction to youth who had been dragged up in the condition of collapsing standards of life as a result of war, one was met by the completely unassailable reply–"Geez! These Wops burn me up!"

As this author records, the US authorities were hell-bent on "reforming" Italian life. Their desire for an end to the Italian Monarchy "was probably the most decisive force in overthrowing the House of Savoy. A new international world was said to be in the process of shaping itself. The Stars and Stripes were bravely fluttering at the head of the column, and all who wanted to feel that they belonged to that brave new world were tempted to fall in and march with it" (Gayre, *op. cit.*, p.42). King Victor Emmanuel III, feeling himself tainted by his association with Mussolini, had abdicated in favor of his son, Umberto II. In 1946, a plebiscite (held by many to be rigged) found a wafer thin majority for a repub- lic. Although there were cries of "treason" on the part of the King's supporters, and the armed forces offered to void the plebiscite, Umberto realized the position of the United States and feared the outcome of a bloody civil war. He went into exile, and an Italian republic, renowned since for its corrup- tion and instability, was called into being.

That this Americanization was not reserved merely for the vanquished but for our Allies as well, may be seen from this quote from the *Catholic Herald* of 6 February 1942:

> Two wars are being waged against England. The first
> we know all about. It is being fought in Europe, in Af-
> rica, in Asia. But the second is no less important and no
> one bothers about it. On this front the outlook is much
> darker. It is the war against the spirit and traditions of
> England, and the enemy lies within our gates. Well may
> German propagandists exclaim that on one side we are
> being Americanised and on the other Sovietised. Open
> any paper or pamphlet, and you will look in vain for a
> mention of "God and My Right," of the ideal of St.
> George, of the Monarchy, of our constitutional heritage,
> of our Christian foundations and Faith, of our litera-
> ture, of our homes that were castles, of our squires, etc.,
> etc., or, if you will find them mentioned, it will generally
> be with an open or veiled sneer.

What 1945 and subsequent years saw, in a nutshell, was
the triumph of Americanism over half the world. The Soviet
menace threw many European Catholic Conservatives completely into our ideological camp, just as before the War it
had pushed many to the Fascists and Nazis. For the most
part, Catholic politicians formed themselves into various
parties of Christian Democrats, accepting electoral democracy and economic liberalism and abandoning the Church's
social teachings to a greater or lesser degree to merit American aid in fending off the Soviets. To a degree this strategy
was echoed even by Pius XII.

The Marshall Plan rushed American aid to the obliter-
ated economies of Western Europe; the North Atlantic Treaty
Organization ensured the presence of large US forces in
Europe to "contain" the Red menace.

But while we maintained our Allies' security in the mother
continent, we cooperated with Communists and local nationalists in ejecting them from their colonial empires. The

most obvious example of this was in the Dutch East Indies. There, the Netherlands attempted to restore their position after the War. Confronted by guerrilla warfare in the colony and American diplomatic and political pressure at home, they gave up after a four year struggle. In 1949, Sukarno presided over the birth of Indonesia. To repay the US for its aid, he followed a steadily pro-Soviet line all the years of his rule. This was the beginning of a pattern which would become drearily familiar over the next two decades.

AT HOME

Many Americans wanted, after V-J Day, simply to return to peace-time patterns. But there could be no return to normalcy. Although initial demobilization was rapid, the result was a recession. Apparently a wartime economy could only conceal the Depression, not exorcise it. The assumption by America of leadership of the Free World and resultant stepping up of production to arm opponents of Communism rescued us from the economic morass of peace. Defense industries became a large sector of the economy, and paved the way for the great boom of the 1950's, a time when America would reach a prosperity unequaled before or since.

At the same time, the threat of Communist infiltration came to the public eye, particularly as their deeds in Eastern Europe and China gradually became better known. In Hollywood, members of the entertainment industry, "blacklisted" for anti-Communism during the War, exposed their confreres with links to the Party. The result was the famous Hollywood Ten case, when a number of such folk perjured themselves regarding their affiliation before a Congressional committee. The famous black lists ensured that many Communists would not work again for years in the industry. What is not so well known is that the careers of those who testified against them were similarly ruined.

Spy cases came to the fore, such as that of Julius and Ethel Rosenberg, who were accused of passing nuclear secrets to the Soviets, thus helping them to acquire the atom bomb and commence a balance of terror which remains with us yet. They were found guilty and later executed, much to the dismay of many who protested their innocence. It is only in recent years that their guilt has been proved by the Russians since the fall of the Soviet Union.

There were voices raised against maintenance of the National Security State created by FDR. Nor were all of these Communists. Such were men like John T. Flynn, true to the same principles he had held when he led the America First Committee. Moreover, the Republican Party was once again in control of Congress after the 1946 elections (in similar wise as their success after World War I). But the work of FDR had its effect. Where Wilson had had to contend with the likes of Henry Cabot Lodge and Warren Harding, with the Republican Party solidly behind them, the threat of Communism had split the Republicans this time. An interventionist wing of the Party had grown up as a result. Led by Thomas Dewey, its foreign policy was virtually indistinguishable from the Democrats'; in domestic policy it was somewhat less activist, but accepted the huge growth of government Roosevelt had fathered.

Opposed to such people was the more traditional wing of the Party, led by Senator *Robert Taft*. Taft opposed NATO and the UN, using such slogans as "Fortress America," and "The Free Hand." He maintained that acceptance of the permanent role of world policeman could only lead to the loss of liberty at home. He lost the presidential nomination to Dewey in 1948. This signaled (together with Taft's loss again to Eisenhower in 1952) the end of the Republican

Party as a significantly different voice in America.

Truman, Dewey's opponent in that year, had of course been FDR's last Vice President, as well as Grand Master of the Masonic Lodge of Missouri. It was his choice of cities which had led the atom bombs to drop on Hiroshima and Nagasaki (by sheerest coincidence the two centers of Catholicism in Japan). Although the far left and right wings of the Democratic Party each fielded separate candidates in the election, Truman squeezed past Dewey. The man from Independence, Missouri was President in his own right.

Still, the debate about America's place in the world went on, just as it had in 1914 to 1917 and 1939 to 1941. Just as on those occasions, the argument was won, not by reason or appeal to truth, but by force of arms.

The country of Korea, after its liberation from the Japanese, had been divided at the Thirty-eighth parallel between American and Soviet zones in the South and North, respectively. The idea, as in the case of Germany and Austria, was that after a period the halves should be reunited into one democratic Republic of Korea. Each side had their own idea of what those words meant, however, and the result was the establishment of two different governments. By 1949, most American and Soviet troops had been withdrawn. On June 25, 1950, the North invaded South Korea. The UN Security Council, from which the Soviets had walked out, called on all members to assist in repelling this aggression. Two days later, without asking Congress for a declaration of war, Truman ordered US forces into Korea as part of a UN "police action." Where FDR had maneuvered this country into a war without sanction of its people's representatives, Truman simply entered one. As in all our other major wars, the constitution took another beating. At least this time, we were fighting atheists.

ARSENAL OF DEMOCRACY 1952-1969

THE FABULOUS FIFTIES

The War in Korea saw over the two years of its existence the wildest ups and downs, followed by stalemate. After the North Koreans drove the South Koreans and Americans into the small "Pusan Perimeter" in the extreme South-East of the country, they were halted. The perimeter was reinforced massively, and after a counter attack began, the North Koreans were outflanked by the landing at Inchon.

General McArthur was put in command, and soon drove the North Koreans back to the Yalu river, marking the border with China. On November 24, 1950, 180,000 Red Chinese troops poured over the Yalu. By December 15, the UN forces were driven back to the pre-war border of South Korea. Soon, the Reds had captured Seoul, but they were pushed back again, and a stalemate developed.

It was McArthur's desire to carry the war over into Manchuria by bombing Chinese bases there. President Truman, committed as he was to the "containment" of Communism, had no intention of rolling it back. McArthur was fired on April 11, 1951. The stalemate dragged on for two more years, and at last, a truce was negotiated which continues at the time of this writing.

In the meantime, the United States had a new president. The country had been under Democratic rule for almost twenty years, and it was obvious that a Republican would win the White House in 1952. The important question was, what kind of Republican? The traditional wing of the Party was led once again by Senator Taft; the internationalist, interventionist wing, committed to essentially the same foreign and domestic programs as the Democrats, rallied behind General Dwight D. Eisenhower.

Indeed, Eisenhower epitomized all that Americans held most dear; a World War II hero, he gave a feeling of deep-seated comfort, much in keeping with the economic prosperity of the time. Although the public might be tired of the Democrats, they were not really too interested in dismantling the National Security State which had been developed in response to the Depression, World War II, and the Cold War. Above all, Eisenhower reflected the religious sense of the American people:

> The central symbol of the nation's political piety was the President himself. Though not an official church member until after his election, Eisenhower more than made up for this with his frequent religious pronouncements. Ike's faith was a simple one; it was just faith. "Our government makes no sense," he declared during the 1952 campaign, "unless it is founded in a deeply felt religious faith, and I don't care what it is." On another occasion he told the people, though "I am the most intensely religious man I know, that does not mean I adhere to any sect." In still another speech the President assured Americans that this nation was "the mightiest power God has seen fit to put upon his footstool." In 1954, Ike told the nation to spend July Fourth as a day of penance and prayer. He himself went fishing in the morning, played

18 holes of golf in the afternoon, and bridge at night
(Douglas T. Miller and Marion Nowak, *The Fifties*, p.90).

Peace and prosperity made such cant sound good. It certainly was a time of prosperity for this nation, unequaled
either before or since. Most American families could eat meat
every night of the week. They could realistically plan to live
well, travel on vacations, save for their retirement, and plan
to pay for their children's college. Automobile ownership
soared, and huge gas-guzzling machines, tail-finned to reflect the atomic age, roared down the nation's highways.

Above all, the 1950's were the Golden Age of Television.
The new medium mushroomed throughout the country,
until by the end of the decade the vast majority of households were equipped with them. It was and is a powerful
tool. So compelling was it that whereas before its advent many
activities competed for people's leisure time, afterwards it
was always a question of doing anything else or watching
TV. The viewpoint of the majority was shaped by what they
saw on the tube, something which would have tremendous
effects in American public life.

More and more, politicians and other public figures tai-
lored their actions and speech to the TV cameras. TV news
more and more came to shape reality as well as to report it.
Where in the beginning, television situation comedies
("sitcoms") served to reinforce conformity (à la *Father Knows
Best, Make Room for Daddy, Leave it to Beaver,* and *Ozzie and
Harriet*), in time, all sorts of perverse behavior would be
popularized and made acceptable thereon.

On a more tangible note, the center of family life shifted
from the dinner-table or the fire place to the black box. Fro-
zen TV dinners saved housewives time for important view-
ing. Even local cultures in such places as Pennsylvania and
Louisiana were threatened, as time spent chatting with neigh-

bors in the evenings in Pennsylvania Dutch or Cajun French were replaced with sitting passively in front of the English-spouting tube. In America and all over the globe, singing in pubs was replaced with gawking at ball-games on the bar TV.

There developed also a particular world for children. The Baby Boom carried on through the last half of the '40's all the way to 1960. In the face of vast numbers of children, kiddie shows on television (like *The Mickey Mouse Club, Howdy Doody,* and *Davy Crockett*) echoed the creation of ever more child-oriented amusement spots, like Disneyland.

If there was a keynote to the '50's, it was homogeneity. Business was good, and America was the wealthiest and most powerful nation in the world. Anyone who thought otherwise might well be a Communist.

And yet, there were Communists about. Senators *Joseph McCarthy* and *Hamilton Fish, Sr.* conducted a campaign against Communists in government via the Senate Government Operations Committee. While they did indeed turn up many well-concealed Reds, their often slipshod methods laid them open to charges of impropriety. At last, McCarthy got into a dispute with the Army leadership. The result was predictable: he was censured by the Senate on December 2, 1954. From that day until the demise of the Soviet Union, any opponent of Communism was liable to be called a "McCarthyite," who indulged in "McCarthyism."

The Soviet Union's acquisition of the atom bomb added to the strange atmosphere of fear which co-existed with the national mood of self-congratulation. The prospect of atomic war led to the proliferation of home bomb shelters, of "drop and cover" drills in schools, and air raid sirens in the rapidly proliferating suburbs. In these synthetic living spaces, the '50's achieved their epitome.

Education fell ever more under the influence of the ideas

of *John Dewey* (1859-1952), last of the triad of great American educators (Horace Mann and Noah Webster being the other two). He carried their ideas even further. Education was no longer to be about imparting literacy at all; rather, it was primarily intended as a means of socialization, a way of integrating the pupil into the educator's vision of what society should be. Although various voices were raised throughout the '50's to protest the progressive de-emphasis on academic skills, such protests came to nothing in the end. Public education in the US would become woefully inadequate, although it did manage to contribute to the destruction of morality among the young.

Despite it all, the image of the '50's remained "The Man in the Gray Flannel Suit": the martini drinking, back-yard barbecuing, association-joining 1950's successor to Babbitt. His sons and daughters were in the scouts, attended dutifully with their parents the church of their parents' choice, and enjoyed the standard-of-living their fathers bestowed on them—a standard far in advance (as he was always happy to tell them) of his during the Depression. Trick-or-treating for UNICEF, watching TV shows, and going off to summer camp were some of their rituals. Surely, this new generation, better educated and better fed than any which preceded it, would be happy and glad to inherit and continue the manner of life their parents would leave them. Time would tell.

VOICES OF DISSENT

Not everyone was convinced that Americans lived in the best of all possible worlds. On a lighter note, *MAD Magazine*, with its non-stop parody of American life, soared to popularity among the young. But not everyone was content merely to poke fun at American mores.

American ideological Conservatism, in the sense of a real

intellectual alternative to Eisenhower Republicanism, appeared to be virtually dead after his election. Conservatism, in the sense of attachment to the status quo was of course dominant. But of a conscious opposition to the New Deal and its heirs, there seemed to be none when Eisenhower was inaugurated.

Nevertheless, that very year there appeared a remarkable book by a remarkable man: *The Conservative Mind, From Burke to Santayana*, by *Russell Kirk*. This survey of foreign and American right-wing thought, brought together in an attempt to find some commonality between them, marked a change in American ideas. For Kirk, an admirer of Edmund Burke, there *was* a connection between Anglo-American Whiggery and both the Euro-Latin American Right and Southern Agrarianism. An admirer of the English system, Kirk nevertheless maintained that the American Revolution was a development of the British Glorious one, and like that event essentially a "Conservative happening."

But Kirk was responsible for bringing to the attention of the American public such folk as Roy Campbell, the South African Catholic convert poet who had fought for Franco. A few years later, young *William F. Buckley, Jr.,* author of the 1951 *God and Man at Yale* (which exposed the "anti-Americanism" of the Ivy League colleges), founded the magazine *National Review.* At its inception, it was reminiscent of Seward Collins' *American Review*, and provided space for such as the surviving Southern Agrarians and John Flynn.

European writers like *Erik von Kuehnelt-Leddihn* and *Thomas Molnar* were given place, as were native Americans like *Frederick Wilhelmsen* and *L. Brent Bozell*. Save Kirk (who would later convert) all these men were Catholics, although many other contributors to NR were not. In any case, throughout the '50's and into the next decade, the magazine provided the most cogent criticism of the status quo the non-Catholic press offered. But it could not solve the abiding problem of American Conservatism: the revolutionary nature of the very national fabric American Conservatives wished to conserve. The strain would show later.

In the meantime, the newly resurgent Conservative movement focused upon several problems with contemporary America. Southern Agrarian sorts kept up their criticisms of the ever more centralized state; such as John Flynn likewise carried on their crusade against the decay of constitutional government. Similar in outlook, the opposition of the first group of men was based on cultural grounds, the second on political.

More English-oriented sorts took the whole notion of Democracy to task, declaring that the "Republic" of the Founding Fathers was aristocratic rather than democratic. These kinds of people attacked the whole American mythology of the virtue of the "masses." The Conservative virtues of anti-ideologism and preservation of continuity were praised continually by these folk, chief of whom was Kirk.

The criticisms of Catholics involved with the movement were often even more to the point. In *Liberty or Equality?*, Erik von Kuehnelt-Leddihn argued that these two qualities were incompatible, the quest for equality bringing forth both Nazism and Communism. Thomas Molnar argued in *The Counterrevolution* that lack of conviction on the part of the Right was responsible for the victory of the Left, more than any other single factor: the Left believed in what it was doing. The Carlist supporter, Frederick Wilhelmsen, was a stout defender of Catholic social teachings, without any nod to Americanism. Not surprisingly, these men were all Monarchists; just as unsurprisingly, they had little connection, despite their religion, with most American Catholics, whether clerical or lay.

The one thing which truly united these folk to one another and to the remaining Taft Republicans was their common opposition to Communism, which at the time looked about ready to swallow the earth. That message was listened to; but their espousal of excellence against the complacent conformity of the majority fell on deaf ears at a time when the White House was occupied by its most popular holder—who happened to be, in appearance, habits, and beliefs, a dead ringer for Babbitt.

Another, and seemingly diametrically opposed field of dissent was that of the "Beat" movement. Like the more Europeanized wing of the Conservative movement, the "Beats" rebelled against the dull, gray, conformism of the '50's—which, after all, was only standard American Calvinism made triumphant over the world by victory in the Second World War. Featuring in its number such odd folk as *William Burroughs, Allen Ginsberg, Lawrence Ferlinghetti,* and *Gregory Corso,* the Beat Generation's solutions to the dryness and deadness of American life were often bizarre, to say the least, and involved a great deal of incoherent poetry, "alternative" life-styles, unemployment, Eastern religions, drugs, and alcohol. In a word, they offered rebellion, pure and simple.

Yet all the evil, squalor, and plain looniness encompassed by the Beats ought not to blind the observer to the fact that much of the criticism of American society which they expressed was quite valid:

> The Beats, and such literary fellow travelers as the Black Mountain poets, shared a unity of purpose. They all wished to restore literature and the arts to the people, to bring literature back from its dull sleep of obscure academic poems and alienated, apathy-inducing novels. Many of the most important Beat works themselves reflect a deep alienation from American society: *Howl's* denunciations of materialism and sexual repression, and

the scorn for the middle class in *On The Road*, are only two instances. The romantic fascination with criminality that permeated much of Beat life also was a sign of its estrangement. But these were not simply statements of alienation. The Beats went beyond alienation to emphasize the need for a new American community. They tried to burst through (rather than simply reflect) a world of deadening politics, sexual hypocrisy, TV-induced numbness. As Allen Ginsberg would later put it, the Beat movement meant "the return to nature and the revolt against the machine....it's either that or take that mass-produced self they keep trying to shove down your throat" (Miller and Nowak, *op. cit.*, p.384).

If their solutions were mad, the problems they posed were not. Indeed, many of their criticisms of American society (save the sexual ones; this is an area where folk are always likely to confuse chastity with repression—they are in fact as different as temperance and prohibition) would have seemed quite apparent to Southern Agrarians or to the Euro-Conservatives. But with the partial exception of the latter, the Beats shared with Conservatives one major blind spot: they would or could not see that the solution lay ultimately in the conversion of America to the Catholic Faith; that Catholicism alone could reconcile order and liberty, art and life. But in large part this was due to the distorted Americanist Catholicism which they saw around them.

All of this is made manifest in the life of the most interesting of the Beatniks, *Jean-Louis (Jack) Kerouac* (1922-1969). Born and raised a French-speaker in Lowell, Massachusetts, and author of *On The Road*, Kerouac left Lowell at the age of 17. First joining the Merchant Marine during World War II, he eventually studied for a time at Columbia University (where he met Ginsberg) before publishing his first novel in 1950. After that he began his vagabond-like existence. But apart from the snatches of French he often uses in his novels, his religious and cultural upbringing at once separated him from mainstream America, and sparked the mysticism (including, alas, a fascination with Buddhism) which marked most of his literary career.

For a man of his type, there can be no doubt that the immigrant community in which he was raised was terribly confining; yet it is just as obvious that his flirtation with the East and his joining "a widespread subterranean culture of poets, folk singers, hipsters, mystics, and eccentrics..." (*Encyclopedia Britanica*) were attempts to find, once more as an adult, the Faith and folk he had known through a child's perceptions. Certainly, in his last few years he became quite Conservative indeed; many of his utterances would not have been out of place in the pages of Fr. Lionel Groulx's *Action Française Canadienne.* At any rate, although he died in Florida, he was buried from his childhood parish in Lowell.

Conservatives and Beats alike had little practical influence on the public at large during the '50's, although in the next decade the influence of both groups would dramatically increase. In the meantime, however, one faction did rise to prominence and accomplished several key goals: this was the Civil Rights movement.

As we may recall from previous chapters, blacks in the North generally lived in decaying ghettos; those in the South found their lives circumscribed by the Jim Crow laws. The rhetoric of "freedom and equality" which was bandied about during World War II had the effect of raising hopes among black intellectuals and clergymen that such things would soon be applied to their people. Although Truman ordered the integration of the Army, for the most part blacks and whites dwelt in separate, unequal worlds.

The progressive wing of the Democratic Party assured blacks that, once back in the White House, they would put an end to Jim Crow; Southern Democrats replied that this would not happen. As the decade progressed, the issue of Civil Rights loomed ever larger on the national scene, with Southerners divided over Jim Crow, Conservatives divided over States' Rights, and blacks divided over the best way to bring about change.

For black intellectuals like Ralph Ellison and Richard Wright, it was apparent that forcing an end to Jim Crow and to segregation in general was the only way. Most leadership in the community agreed with them; together with white sympathizers, the result was the Civil Rights movement. But they found themselves faced with opposition: the Conservative Republican, Zora Neale Hurston.

Miss Hurston was bitterly opposed to the Civil Rights movement and its leadership. The reason why is most important:

> Part of Hurston's received heritage–and perhaps the paramount received notion that links the novel of manners in the Harlem Renaissance, the social realism of the thirties, and the cultural nationalism of the Black Arts movement–was the idea that racism had reduced black people to mere ciphers, to beings who only react to an omnipresent racial oppression, whose culture is "deprived" where different, and whose psyches are in the main "pathological." Albert Murray, the writer and social critic, calls this "the Social Science Fiction Monster." Socialists, separatists, and civil rights advocates alike have been devoured by this beast.

> Hurston thought this idea degrading, its propagation a trap, and railed against it. It was, she said, upheld by the "sobbing school of Negrohood who hold that nature somehow has given them a dirty deal." Unlike [Langston] Hughes and Wright, Hurston chose deliberately to ignore this "false picture that distorted..." Free-

dom, she wrote in *Moses, Man of the Mountain,* was something internal...."The man himself must make his own
emancipation." And she declared her first novel a manifesto against the "arrogance" of whites assuming that
"black lives are only defensive reactions to white actions."
Her strategy was not calculated to please (Henry Louis
Gates, Jr., "Afterword," in Zora Neale Hurston, *Mules
and Men,* p.291).

Nor did it; in practice, despite the long term sense of her
beliefs, Miss Hurston's influence would be nil until our own
time.

A major strike for the Civil Rights cause was the decision of the Supreme Court under Chief Justice Earl Warren
(whom we last met packing off the Japanese to camps during
the War) in the case of Brown vs. the Board of Education of
Topeka, Kansas. This verdict, handed down on May 17, 1954
reversed the 1896 Plessy vs. Ferguson ruling, which had permitted "separate but equal" educational facilities. Rather, the
Court found, segregated schools were inherently unequal,
and violated the Fourteenth Amendment, which says that
no state may deny equal protection of the laws to any person
within its jurisdiction.

Meanwhile, the nascent Civil Rights establishment were
gathering strength. A move beyond writing and into action
was the result of an occurrence in Montgomery, Alabama, in
December of 1955. At that time, a middle-aged black woman,
Rosa Parks, refused to give up her seat to a white man and
move to the back of a municipal bus, as was then required.
The black community in the town rallied around Mrs. Parks,
and a boycott of the municipal bus lines was called for, and
led by, a minister named ***Martin Luther King, Jr.***

King, whose birthday is now a national holiday, was an
equivocal figure. Communist or Christian, he set his mark
upon the Civil Rights movement. A Baptist minister, he had

served in his Montgomery church for a year prior to the boycott. A charismatic organizer, he used the action to put together the Southern Christian Leadership Conference, (SCLC). The SCLC was soon in a position to coordinate similar actions throughout the South.

The boycott lasted through 1956; meanwhile the SCLC and the NAACP led anti-segregation drives in hotels, restaurants, schools, and elsewhere.

Opposition was not long in coming, and was motivated by two basic principles. The first was racism pure and simple. Its adherents believed that blacks were inherently inferior and best kept at a distance. The second opposed Jim Crow's abolition out of a belief in States' Rights; that is, they may not have supported Jim Crow, but believed that neither Federal government nor outside opinion had any right to force the majority of a given state's citizens, or their state government, to abolish segregation. Obviously, some individuals were pure racists, other pure States' Righters. But in practice, in varying degrees, the two motives were present in differing proportions in most of the Southern opposition. More respectable people formed the White Citizens' Councils, which were pledged to fighting integration legally and peacefully. The more rif-raffish elements joined the latest incarnation of the Ku Klux Klan.

But the State governments in the South were not unaware of the threat to their sovereignty the Supreme Court decision provided. The year 1956 saw a barrage of action on their parts. On January 19, the Alabama Senate passed a nullification of the Supreme Court's ruling in Brown; a similar "resolution of interposition" was adopted by the Virginia Legislature on February 1; they then closed the Commonwealth's public schools. March 7 saw the same legislature alter the law to allow public aid to private schools. Five days later, 101 Southern representatives and senators published a manifesto calling upon the states to disobey and resist the Supreme Court's ruling by all lawful means.

School segregation was not the only issue at stake. In the South, large numbers of blacks had been effectively disenfranchised around the turn of the century. Having successfully intervened in schooling, the Federal government would deal with the franchise in the South. Despite a filibuster of over 24 hours by South Carolina's Senator Strom Thurmond, Congress passed on August 29 a Civil Rights Bill creating a Commission to investigate denial of voting rights because of religion and race. It further made denial of voting rights in national elections a federal offense.

Meanwhile, the education front was heating up again. After a 1957 ruling by the local US District Court forcing Central High School in Little Rock to integrate, Governor Orval Faubus of Arkansas defied the Court. President Eisenhower in response federalized the Arkansas National Guard and dispatched 1,000 paratroopers to the school on September 24. The next day, nine heavily guarded black schoolchildren began classes. A year later, the Supreme Court ruled that it was the duty of local officials to integrate as soon as possible. On January 19, 1959, the Virginia Supreme Court invalidated the legislature's anti-integration laws; two weeks later, the Norfolk and Arlington schools were integrated peacefully.

Starting in February of 1960, sit-in demonstrations held to desegregate lunch counters and the like were launched throughout the South. Congress passed on April 21 the Civil Rights Act of 1960, despite the 121 hour long filibuster mounted by Southern senators. It allowed Federal authorities to step in whenever they considered state registration practices questionable. By this time, the legal machinery was in place to force the Southern states to accept the abolition of Jim Crow.

What are we to think of all of this? On the one hand, there can be no doubt that Jim Crow encompassed many injustices, indeed. It was not just that blacks were subjected to many indignities on account of race; their natural abilities were stymied artificially, and they simply lacked the opportunity to compete with whites.

However, it also ought to be remembered that Jim Crow was the son of Reconstruction; its notion of basing rights and restrictions upon group membership rather than individual citizenship carried over into Civil Rights legislation. Moreover, the way in which legal segregation was abolished was done by transforming the Supreme Court from an apolitical judicial body into a political quasi-legislative one. It is also interesting to note that since the days of FDR to this, the Supreme Court has only once struck down a Federal law as unconstitutional; rather they have concentrated on State and local measures. Thus it has become a mere instrument for expansion of the Federal prerogative and destruction of State and local autonomy—a patently unconstitutional development

The remaining shreds of States' Rights were destroyed during the Civil Rights controversy. It must be said, that in using them to defend a manifestly unjust system, the Southern politicians showed a criminal blindness. Having lost over integration, there was nothing they could do about fighting abortion, when the time came. Just recently, both Louisiana and Guam fought the Federal government on this key issue. The precedents established in forcing integration were used to beat them down.

CATHOLICISM IN THE 1950's

As noted before, the rise of Communism had forced Pius XII into a *de facto* alliance with the United States. Moreover,

the devastation of World War II had made the American
Church the most important segment (financially) of the
Church as a whole.

A further difficulty was raised by the fact that the Church
had just suffered a great deal under the Nazi and Fascist dic-
tatorships, so many of whose policies had borne a purely
external resemblance to some of the social and economic
teachings of the Church. Above all, having just undergone a
struggle with dictators who forbade dissent, and still suffering under Communists who forbade dissent, many churchmen became enamored of the notions of religious tolerance
and political democracy:

> A Church so schooled in resistance to oppression, re-
> members that it is a Church of the people, rather than of
> rulers; and, whenever it regains its freedom, its tempta-
> tion is to resort to new alliances with popular movements,
> or with parliamentary parties and pressure groups. This
> is the doubtful tendency today of "Catholic Action" and
> of the "Christian Democratic" parties in the new repub-
> lics of Italy, France, and Western Germany (Lord Percy
> of Newcastle, *The Heresy of Democracy*, p.231).

From the Vatican to the local parish, the doctrinal struggle
between Modernism and Orthodoxy, and the socio-cultural
struggle between Americanism and Ultramontanism, was
supplemented by a political struggle between Liberalism and
Traditionalism in terms of separation of Church and State,
rights of unbelievers, and so on.

On the one side in the latter struggle were the generality
of the hierarchies of the United States, France, Germany,
Italy, Belgium and the Netherlands; on the latter, most of
those of Spain, Portugal, and Latin America.

In Spain, the traditional Catholic and monarchical nature of which had been preserved only at the price of a long
and bloody civil war, General Franco had placed in article 6

of the *Fuero de los Españoles*, the country's constitution, the
declaration that: "The profession and practice of the Catholic religion, which is that of the Spanish State, shall enjoy
official protection." The same article went on to say that:
"Nobody shall be molested for his religious beliefs in the
private exercise of his cult. Ceremonies or external manifestations other than those of the Catholic religion will not be
permitted." They would not be permitted to proselytize. By
the terms of the Concordat, teaching in colleges, universities, state and private schools had to conform to Catholicism, and the State would pay clerical salaries and pensions,
as well aiding churches and religious houses financially.

In Salazar's Portugal, separation of Church and State had
been retained in the 1933 Constitution (it having initially
occurred after the revolution of 1910). Divorce was recognized by the State for the marriages of non-Catholics, who
enjoyed religious freedom (including proselytization). But
in the 1940 Concordat, it was agreed that only Catholic ceremonies would be permitted at State functions, and no official government representatives would attend non-Catholic
religious rites.

In Latin America, a number of countries retained something of the ancient organization of Church and State. In
Peru, although civil marriage and divorce were permitted in
1930, article 232 of the 1933 Constitution stated that: "Out
of respect for the sentiments of the majority of the nation,
the State protects the Catholic, Apostolic, and Roman religion. Other religions enjoy freedom for the exercise of their
respective worship." Clergy were forbidden from holding
office, but were exempted from military service; their salaries were paid by the State. The President could present candidates for the episcopate to the Holy See, while Congress
could create or suppress dioceses.

The Panamanian constitution in art. 36 "recognized that

the Catholic religion is that of the majority of Panamanians. It shall be taught in the public schools, but its study and assistance at its acts of worship shall not be obligatory for students, when their parents or guardians so request..." In Paraguay there was constitutional union between Church and State. The Haitian Constitution stated in art. 20: "All the religions and all the denominations recognized in Haiti are free. Everyone has the right to profess his religion and to carry on his form of worship as long as he does not disturb the public order. The Catholic religion, professed by the majority of Haitians enjoys a special position because of the Concordat." In Colombia the Constitution of 1887 in no less than eleven articles detailed the privileges of the Church of which the first sets the tone:

> Art. 1: The Catholic Apostolic Roman Religion is that of the Nation; public authorities will protect it and cause it to be respected as well as its ministers, preserving it in the full exercise of its right and privileges.

In Bolivia also the Catholic Church was the State religion. Argentina's 1947 Constitution required that the President be a Catholic, and required State financing of the Church. In all of these nations, of course, those elements who looked either to New York or Moscow favored separation of Church and State, and continually sought to erode the Church's position.

Such folk had succeeded in Chile, Mexico, Nicaragua, Uruguay, Venezuela, Guatemala, El Salvador, Ecuador, Costa Rica, Honduras, and Brazil–all countries where the anti-clericals had been openly supported by the US.

In all constitutions of those nations which retained the union of Church and State, two separate currents might be seen. In such countries as Colombia, Catholicism was the religion of the State, pure and simple. In others, such as Peru and Panama, that recognition was based solely on the fact that the Faith was professed by the majority of citizens. There was a subtle but important difference: in the first case, Catholicism being true, it simply *is* the religion of the State. In the second, that status is based solely upon the will of the people. The Irish case shows the consequences of these differences.

The Irish Constitution of 1937 stated the following in "Article 44: Religion":

> 1. The State acknowledges that the homage of public worship is due to almighty God. It shall Hold his name in reverence, and shall respect and honor religion.

> 2. The State recognizes the special position of the Holy Catholic Apostolic and Roman Church as the guardian of the Faith professed by the great majority of the citizens.

> 3. The State also recognizes the Church of Ireland, the Presbyterian Church in Ireland, the Methodist Church in Ireland, the Religious Society of Friends in Ireland, as well as the Jewish congregations and the other religious denominations existing in Ireland at the date of the coming into operation of this Constitution.

By American standards, this is a rather radical statement, as indeed those in all the constitutions we have just looked at are. But from an integrally Catholic point of view, it is not so. During the 1950's, there flourished in Ireland an organization called *Maria Duce*, organized by the redoubtable Fr. Denis Fahey, whom we met with during the Depression. In the *Irish Times* of March 7, 1950, J.P. Ryan, Secretary of *Maria Duce*, critiqued Article 44 from a purely Catholic viewpoint:

> For a Catholic, religion is a matter of dogmatic certi-

tude. For him there is only one true religion. In consequence, all non-Catholic sects, as such, are false and evil, irrevocably so. While a Catholic must always respect the non-Catholics' personal rights and liberty of conscience, he may never regard their beliefs as other than false, "may never connive in any way at false opinions, never withstand them less zealously than the truth allows" (Leo XIII). For a Protestant, on the other hand, religion is a matter of private judgment, a question of opinion. Moreover, since no Protestant claims the prerogative of personal infallibility (as Catholics do for the Pope in matters of faith and morals), it is evident that for a Protestant, thus deprived of dogmatic certainty, the only sane attitude towards those who disagree with his religious opinions is to regard such opinions with a certain respectful deference. Hence the Protestant notion of "religious toleration," the "one-religion-is-as-good-as-another" philosophy which is the logical outcome of private judgment. Toleration for a Catholic always implies that what is tolerated is an evil, and that the toleration of this evil is itself justified only when such toleration is necessary to avoid a greater evil—that is, it is justified by the application of the principle of the double effect. Religious toleration for the Protestant, on the contrary, has no such implications. It is merely the "broadminded," "liberal," admission that people are entitled to their opinions.

What then must be the attitude of Catholic States, such as Spain and Ireland, towards Protestantism and non-Catholic sects in general? The ideal (as outlined in the Syllabus of Pius IX, *Ubi Arcano* and *Quas Primas* of Pius XI) is that the Catholic State, while extending full liberty and official recognition to the Catholic Church alone, should not only not connive at the proselytism of non-Catholic sects, but should suppress them as inimical to the common good. This attitude is quite logical,

since for a Catholic State the vitality of Catholic life is
the chief good of society. Such intolerance of error is the
privilege of truth. Nor does it entail any violence to the
liberty of the individual conscience, for "the Church is
wont to take earnest care that no one shall be forced to
embrace the Catholic Faith against his will." (Leo XIII,
Immortale Dei).

Nowadays, however, this ideal, such as was realized
in Catholic Spain under Ferdinand and Isabella, is not
encountered in practice. In many countries predominantly
Catholic, the Church, while never abdicating one iota of
her sacred rights, is, nevertheless, obliged to be content
with an imperfect recognition. In such circumstances the
suppression by the State of falsehood and false sects, however desirable, is not feasible. The principle of toleration
(in the Catholic sense already explained) may then be
invoked as a temporary expedient, a concession to ad-
verse circumstances, by no means a compromise with
error itself. The principle is explicitly laid down by Leo
XIII in *Immortale Dei*. There it is clear that this toleration is justified only when the Catholic State in question, while extending official recognition to the Catholic
Church alone, has a proportionately grave reason for
permitting the evil of heresy to survive within its bor-
ders.

We proceed to point out that the liberalism of Article
44 of the Constitution stands unequivocally condemned
for giving equal recognition to all forms of religious belief, since it is contrary to reason and revelation alike
that error and truth should have equal rights (Leo XIII).
From repeated Papal pronouncements, it is abundantly
clear that the Catholic Church not only does not con-
done, but vigorously condemns, the much-vaunted "toleration" of most modern constitutions.

That this kind of talk sounds radical to us is a measure of

how far we have fallen from Catholic principles. But the fear of *Maria Duce* of the Irish Constitution's liberalism was duly demonstrated by subsequent events. Even the modest recognition given the Church was removed from the text in 1976, the referendum campaign being fought under the notion that such a move was necessary if Ireland was to "catch up" with the rest of the Common Market, which the country had joined three years previously. Catholic influence waned until the first half of the 1990's saw the nation's history textbooks ignoring most of the contribution of the Faith to Irish culture, and implying that the privations suffered by the Irish during the Penal Times were mythical. The President was a pro-abortion feminist named Mary Robinson, who in turn was married to a Protestant gentleman who happened to be a high-ranking Freemason. Most telling (if purely symbolic) was the fact that in the early 1990's, Dublin Castle, symbol of rule in Ireland, saw its Chapel Royal (Anglican until 1942, when it was made over into the Catholic Church of the Holy Trinity) turned in the latest renovation into a non-denominational chapel.

Even in countries where the hierarchy supported Liberalism, large numbers of layfolk and some priests continued to profess the Catholic traditions of that nation. Many of these in France were aroused by the struggle over Algeria, of which more shortly. A hostile American commentator said of such folk:

> The Church has many chapels; one of them preserves the memories of the *ancien régime*. Its old saints are De Maistre, Chateaubriand, Albert de Mun; its latter-day saint, Charles Maurras. Not Maritain. The worshippers are of all age groups and professions, military and civilians. We find there Alphonse Juin, the marshal, and an old acquaintance, General Chassin. There is also General Jouhaud. Not all the faithful can attend, but they

send flowers: Generals Zeller and Salan, De Beaufort, De Bonneval, and Gardy; many more. All the king's men in their uniforms, and next to them, the members of the other army in *their* uniform: the cloth.

Meet the Other France, attempting, once more, to convert This France. The sacred language fills the room with irresistibly majestic sounds; the visions of the saints, the words of great churchmen are recalled with loving care. But listen closely, and you hear the guns of the Algerian war sound through the thunder from Mount Sinai. *Propaganda fide* blends with the theories of revolutionary war: the army must be given a good conscience (James H. Meisel, *The Fall of the Republic*, p.244).

Despite his mocking tone, the truth of their position emerges; these were folk whose Faith inspired them to fight for Catholic order, in this case in France and Algeria.

Nor were this sort of people lacking elsewhere. In Italy, the great Catholic philosopher of history, *Attilio Mordini* (1923-1966) and his disciples went so far as to "reject the Risorgimento and exalt the Habsburgs as heirs of the Holy Roman Empire." Similar views were espoused by the *Neues Abendland* group:

> There is a castle in South Württemberg, near Liechtenstein, the Schloss Zeil, the ancestral home of the princely family of Waldburg-Zeil, which is the headquarters of a group calling itself *Neues Abendland*, and the honorary President is the Archduke Otto of Habsburg. The word *Abendland* generally signifies Christian Europe as against the *Morgenland* of the pagan East, and was used as early as the Crusades. In its present particular context it means a land which preserves European monarchist traditions and virtues, especially the Catholic virtues, against the Russian and conceivably even the American menace (Bocca, *op. cit.*, p.136).

Despite the fact that such folk faced opposition from both their bishops and most of the leadership of their respective national Christian Democratic parties, their very existence was a testimony to the continuing power of the Catholic tradition.

In America, things were a bit different, as we shall see presently. But occasionally, a Catholic would stand up against "the American Way." In January of 1953, for example:

> Anna Collazo, an employee of the Puerto Rican Department of Education, refused to swear allegiance to the entire constitution. She would defend all the laws of the Commonwealth, she said, except those opposed to divine law. Father Arroyo, director of the Confraternity of Christian Doctrine, defended her action, declaring it the duty of all Catholics to make a mental or written reservation against birth control, sterilization, and the secularist school laws when pledging to defend the Puerto Rico commonwealth laws (1954 *Catholic Almanac*, p.717).

Little enough, one might say, when weighed against all that Catholics were doing elsewhere at that time. But for the United States, it was just the sort of thing to unleash a new wave of anti-Catholicism.

Already, in 1947, Chicago's Methodist Temple played host on November 20 to the founding of an organization with the catchy title, Protestants and Other Americans United For Separation of Church and State (POAU). Its founders drew their membership from Protestant groups, Scottish Rite Freemasonry, the National Education Association, humanist societies, and the American Jewish Congress:

> The "big three" of the founding fathers were Glenn L. Archer of the NEA; Paul Blanshard, a Congregationalist minister and former employee of the US State De-

partment; and the last, C. Stanley Howell, a Methodist minister. Archer called the Catholic Church a tyranny behind the purple curtain of Roman clericalism; Blanshard described Catholicism as "a dictatorial society within America's democratic society"; and Lowell averred that a Catholic education might qualify a person for citizenship in a totalitarian society but not a free country, adding that "I do not want my child in a school directed by officials who are under control of a foreign potentate" (Hurley, *op. cit.*, p.35).

Throughout the '50's, POAU would keep up a steady assault against the Church, and particularly against her schools, which John Dewey described as "inimical to democracy." Having dropped "Protestant" from the title, AU soldiers on in our own time.

Rather more successful (both in getting a hearing and raking in the cash), Paul Blanshard continued his crusade via book writing. In his first effort, *American Freedom and Catholic Power* (1949), Blanshard outlined the "Catholic problem" as he saw it:

> There is no doubt that the American Catholic hierarchy has entered the political arena, and that it is becoming more and more aggressive in extending the frontiers of Catholic authority into the fields of medicine, education and foreign policy. In the name of religion, the hierarchy fights birth-control and divorce laws in all states. It tells Catholic doctors, nurses, judges, teachers, and legislators what they can and cannot do in many of the controversial phases of their professional conduct. It segregates Catholic children from the rest of the community in a separate school system and censors the cultural diet of these children. It uses the political power of some thirty-five million official American Catholics to bring American foreign policy into line with Vatican temporal interests (p.2).

But the Catholic problem is still with us. Primarily it
is not the problem of assimilation of the Catholic *people*;
they have been absorbed into the American community
as completely as could be expected in view of the attitude of their priests. Essentially the Catholic problem in
America is what to do with the hierarchy of the Roman
Church. The American Catholic *people* have done their
best to join the rest of America, but the American Catholic
hierarchy, as we shall see in the course of this survey, has
never been assimilated. It is still fundamentally Roman
in its spirit and directives (pp.13-14).

This was followed by a whirlwind of tracts exposing
Catholic crimes against freedom in Spain, Portugal, and Ireland. Blanshard's tactic was to examine Papal and other documents (like the quote from J.P. Ryan above) and to presume
that they represented the goals of the American hierarchy
for this country, thus subjugating the States to a dictatorship
equally as bad as Communism. In this analysis he made two
major errors.

The first was that the American ethos he rightly saw
Catholicism as threatening was worth defending. This was
the dry, conformist horror the Beats so decried; this was
Babbittry. It comprised freedom for heresy, which must always mean slavery for Truth; freedom for divorce, contraception, abortion and sterilization—in a word, freedom to
wallow in the mire of degradation. This was what Blanshard
equated with America, and hated the Church for trying to
prevent.

His second error was in supposing that the American
Churchmen really wanted to save their countrymen from
this fate. There were some few who did, to be sure; but
Americanism was ever more triumphant, and found its latest champion in one *Fr. John Courtney Murray, S.J.*

Fr. Murray, tried in numerous books and articles (such

as *We Hold These Truths*) to prove that the Americanist ideology, particularly in the Constitution, actually enshrined Catholic principles, rather than denying them. At first (in response to Blanshard) obliquely, and then ever more boldly, he declared that separation of Church and State on the American model was superior to the traditional concept of Church establishment. He soon came into conflict with Msgr. Joseph Fenton, editor of the *American Ecclesiastical Review* who defended the traditional view. These two would carry on the fight throughout the '50's.

From merely defending the American separation of Church and State as a legitimate good, Murray's thought, as it developed, became ever more radical. He came to positively despise old Christendom in words fitting for Bishop O'Connell in 1898: "Catholicism in turn now feels that certain of its past unities were something of a scandal; we now reject, for instance, the specious unity asserted in Belloc's famous thesis that 'Europe is the faith and the faith is Europe.'" He then came to affirm the rights of the individual as being superior to the rights of Truth:

> ...it is granted at the outset that rights may not be founded on error, but only on truth. The first immediate affirmation, however, is that rights are inherent in persons. Rights are founded on the dignity of the person, which is the first truth of the social order–the order in which rights are affirmed and exercised. The dignity of the person is a basic constituent element of the objective moral order, the order on which society itself and its laws and processes must be based.

Thus, based upon his dignity as a person, every man had the inherent right to choose error for himself. Just as the American Republic, by ignoring God and religion in its constitution practically denied that public life could be touched by questions of the supernatural order, Murray would have

the Church regard the individual in the same way, looking
not at his eternal end, but at his temporal state.

But Murray was not a revolutionary; he was simply ar-
ticulating that which had been the working doctrine of the
American Church for a long time.

It was a hard doctrine to argue with, simply because the
American Church under its guidance had become so wealthy
and successful; not merely in terms of churches, religious
houses, schools, universities, and hospitals, but in associa-
tions as well. From the Knights of Columbus to the Auto
League of the Sacred Heart, there were organizations designed to appeal to Catholics of every interest. There were
books and magazines published, and all sorts of goings on.
Nor were the spiritual elements neglected: mass Eucharistic
and rosary rallies testified to the strength of Catholic senti-
ment in such places as Boston, New York, Chicago, and San
Francisco. *Archbishop Fulton Sheen's* TV show was extremely
popular: its comforting and non-denominational message that
"Life is worth living," consoled but did not challenge.

Such was Catholic growth that Blanshard and his cro-
nies grew ever shriller. They might have saved their breath.
For the average Catholic in the '50's was interested purely
and simply in sharing the general prosperity and conformity.
People flocked, for example, to the morning Masses of those
priests who could rattle off the Tridentine Mass in 15 min-
utes. As among Protestants, holiness and respectability were
seen as interchangeable qualities, and anything beyond making money a waste of time. Religion was important merely
as a moral system, rather than a means of grace, of transcen-
dence, of eternal ecstasy. The Church's only function, really,
was to serve as cheerleader for secular change; hence, when
the Archbishop of New Orleans illegally (in terms of Canon
Law) excommunicated Judge Leander Perez and several other
layfolk for their opposition to integration in schools, he was

hailed as "far sighted" (although the POAU crowd did not loudly object to this particular intervention of a bishop in politics, oddly enough).

There were some noteworthy attempts, however, to lead a fully Catholic life. The Catholic Worker and the Madonna and Friendship Houses continued, of course. But in 1946, Carol Robinson and Ed Willock founded *Integrity* Magazine.

In the decade it survived, *Integrity* raised important questions, and pricked the conscience of Catholic America. In one of its most powerful articles, it addressed the national ideology which Blanshard defended:

> The prevailing practical philosophy of Americans is liberalism. Since its spirit pervades the very atmosphere we live in it is not surprising that most Catholics are practical liberals in their daily lives.
>
> Think of liberalism as a vacuum, a chaos where men are guided by principles of expediency rather than absolute morality, as absence of order, as inconclusive and indeterminate, and you get its mark. It served to destroy the Christian order, not by contradicting it so much as by diluting and confusing it, by nullifying it at every turn. For the Christian absolute it did not substitute another absolute, but an absence of any absolute, an indeterminism, a tolerance of good and evil, truth and untruth, not in a prudential way, as allowing certain evils to exist rather than stir up worse evils in trying to eradicate them, but as not really preferring one to another. Liberalism used good words ambiguously, so that gradually they were drained of their Christian implications and then gradually again were charged with meaning antithetical to Christianity. It enshrined liberty, equality, and fraternity, but as ultimates, not as means and not as byproducts of absolute things such as truth and goodness, not as related to morality but as isolated from God. It

worshipped democracy, which is only a means of government, which depends on basic ideals for its real worth.
It talked endlessly about freedom, and it was easy to persuade people that this was the same freedom that Christians cherish, but was it? Christ said, "You shall know
the truth, and the truth shall make you free." His freedom is a result of knowing the truth—the result of what
the liberals like to call "intolerance" and "dogmatism."
The liberal's freedom is quite different. It is the freedom
to search for truth. Of course, it is a good thing for the
men who do not know the Truth to be able to look for it.
The trouble with the liberals is that they will not let anyone find it. If anyone claims to find it, he becomes an
outcast from their society. They are, it turns out, dogma-
tists in their own curious way. They know there is no
truth, or if there is, it's not knowable.

We have a liberal government, without any real principles, paying lip service to God, and talking more and
more about democracy and freedom, while both of these
are vanishing for lack of roots in something deeper. We
have, or did have until a few years ago (things are rapidly
changing), a system in this country of liberal economics,
which meant free competition and the legal right to abuse
the moral right of private property. It also involved freedom from sanctions against usury. Our system of free
compulsory education is also, or was until recently, liberal. Liberal means undogmatic, which means remaining undecided about all the important truths (except that
one is allowed his private opinion) while attaching an
exaggerated importance and a thousand dogmas to matters of art, literature, science, hygiene, and civics.

The effect of liberalism, economic, philosophical, and
cultural, over a period of centuries, has been to destroy
all norms. It has no moral code of its own and has en-
dured only as long as Christian morals have survived to
hold society together—not only Christian morals but

Christian standards of all sorts. The end of liberalism had to be dog-eat-dog because the philosophy itself has no backbone, nothing wherein to construct a life or society. We are in the last stages of it now, and we find everything in ruins. Western society, indeed the whole world, has become one great big vacuum, one vastness empty of all positive content (Carol Robinson, *My Life With Thomas Aquinas*, pp.34-35).

Quite a powerful passage, indeed! Yet, should anyone consider such a message too negative, this reply on the part of the magazine's editors might be instructive:

When accused of negativism, we used to object that to see that the world is ordered against Christ is at least to see something, and that it is so far true. It is better, for instance, than saying a bad thing is a good thing, just to be cheerful. Yet if our readers are to make over society, we need to see through the disaster to God's use of this adversity, through the modern despair to the hope that lies in Christ. Hope doesn't lie anywhere else except in Christ. That is the vision which is becoming blinding. That is the only source of a "positive viewpoint." The only constructive program is toward a Christ-centered society. We were right, we think, not to have lavished flattery on any scheme whatever from which the supernatural has been strained out, or to which the Redemption was accidental. We now see, dimly, but certainly, that our elevation to the order of grace must act as the integrating principle in the transformation of the world (*Integrity*, 1949, vol.3, no.2).

As might be expected, this vision led them out of the editorial office and into the world—or more exactly, back to the land. Ed Willock and a number of other like-minded men, mostly Irish Catholics from the Bronx, decided they wanted to put their beliefs into action. In 1949 a tract of land was found where the dream might be carried out. A

parcel of rural land was found in West Nyack, in then-rural
Rockland County about twenty miles northwest of the Bronx.
For $600 apiece, heads of families were entitled to one acre
homesteads and corporate ownership of a large common field
where cattle might be herded and grain raised. Although the
settlers would build their own homes, an architect and a
master builder were hired to give advice.

By the late 1950's, some twelve families were settled, with
79 children. Inspired by Fr. Francis X. Weiser's excellent series of books detailing Catholic paraliturgical customs, they
set to work to lead a truly Catholic life. Willock wrote later:
"It matures a man to drive hundreds of nails, lay hundreds
of bricks, erect hundreds of studs, apply hundreds of
shingles...persons who create together will learn to re-create
together and even pray together....Marycrest was the scene
of rich paraliturgical ceremony: the fields were blessed by
local priests; the entire community gathered for Christian
folksinging under the light of the moon; bonfires were lit on
St. John's Eve." The settlers were pledged to voluntary poverty.

But in the end, most of the children drifted away, and
the original drive was lost. Why? Because it is never enough
for Catholics simply to withdraw from the world. The level
of dependence that techno-industrial man has on the system
around him forced the Marycresters to interact with the sur-
rounding hostile society to a still-significant extent—thus
bringing before the children the stark contrast between it
and their parent's para-liturgical revival in such a way as to
suggest that there was something unreal, artificial, about the
latter. After some time, Marycrest was assimilated.

Those who adopt a "fortress mentality" against the outside world, as if a safe "plastic bubble" of genuine Catholicism could flourish behind the fortress walls, attempt a dangerous strategy in the long run. Such enclaves can indeed be

"plastic"–artificial–if their Catholic youth are not trained to survive and grow, Faith-wise, in a hostile world that they, children of techno-society that they are, can not ever really live independently of.

The crowning moment of American Catholic assimilation was the 1959 declaration of Massachusetts Senator John F. Kennedy, then in the running for the Presidential election to be held the next year, before the Houston Ministerial Association. In front of that august body, he solemnly promised that his religion would not affect his conduct in office. Thus did the man who shortly would be the country's best known Catholic layman agree to give up his freedom of religion, the integrity of his Faith, to gain the whole world–or at least the presidency of these United States.

FOREIGN POLICY IN THE AGE OF EISENHOWER

To this day, the legend of Eisenhower's stalwart anti-Communism has survived intact. His secretary of state, *John Foster Dulles*, had his method of dealing with the Soviets dubbed by the Press, "brinksmanship" (implying that he would bring the country to the brink of war, if necessary). Certainly, there is much to justify this view at first glance.

Eisenhower not only ended the Korean War, but aided the French financially in their struggle to keep Indochina free of Communism. In 1954, he dispatched troops to Guatemala to assist in the overthrow of a pro-Communist regime there. The next year, he rushed support to the Nationalist Chinese on Taiwan when the Reds threatened invasion and did in fact seize the Tachen islands offshore. In 1956, his administration joined with Great Britain, France, Australia, New Zealand, Pakistan, the Philippines, and Thailand in forming the South East Asia Treaty Organization

(SEATO), which hoped to play the part of NATO in its region. Similarly, he lent a benevolent eye to the Baghdad Pact (later the Central Treaty Organization–CENTO) which united Great Britain, Turkey, Iraq, Iran, and Pakistan for the same cause, thus completing a circle of anti-Communist organizations around the periphery of the Communist world.

On March 7, 1957, Congress approved the "Eisenhower Doctrine," which declared American aid and troops would be sent anywhere in the Middle East where called upon by a country threatened by Communist aggression. Under its provisos, 5,000 marines were dispatched to Lebanon in July of 1958, at the same time that the King of Iraq was overthrown and murdered by army officers (his cousin, the King of Jordan, called in British troops to escape that fate).

So from that time on, we have been used to thinking of Eisenhower as a "Cold Warrior." But the reality was somewhat different. As intimated before, the interest of the United States government was not rolling back the Iron Curtain; nor was its policy elsewhere affected by considerations other than dynamiting its allies from their overseas possessions and influence:

> The process of decolonization after World War II was accelerated under the prod of America. The United States was staking out its own self-interested position in the world, at times unavoidably at odds with Britain and France. The country was in its ascendancy, flexing its power, testing its limits, and finding them seemingly nonexistent. It was, exulted Henry Luce in his mass publications, *Time, Life,* and *Fortune,* "the American Century." Americans did not disagree, nor did European colonialists, though most of them were not happy about it, for each new country that emerged was one less bauble on the glittering necklace of empire, another shock to the once mighty power and prestige of Britain and France.

British Foreign Secretary Selwyn Lloyd expressed some of the resentment that Europeans felt in the mid-1950's in his memoirs written two decades later. "The Americans were, on the face of it, loyal and dependable allies but underneath there were in many Americans' hearts a dislike of colonialism, a resentment of any authority left to us from the great days of our empire, and a pleased smile, only half concealed, at seeing us go down" (Donald Neff, *Warriors at Suez*, p.19).

This led us to grease the skids, so to speak, for the British in Cyprus and East Africa, for the French in North Africa, and for the Belgians in the Congo. It led Eisenhower to assure the British and French of his support when they were engaging the Egyptians (in tandem with Israel) over Nasser's seizure of the Suez Canal in 1956, only to turn against them when the Soviets threatened war. Afterwards, Britain would never defy US policy again, becoming a sort of satellite. But in France, the resulting instability led to the overthrow of the Fourth Republic and the ascent of De Gaulle two years later. Although he in turn betrayed his military sponsors by giving away Algeria, he would defy Washington by pulling France out of NATO rather than give up control to the US of her nuclear arsenal in 1965.

This anti-colonial bias did no one any good. It weakened our allies, of course; but the regimes which replaced them were unstable, and despots often came to power who at once made their peoples' lives miserable, and opened their nations to Soviet influence. But in destroying what remained of these empires, Eisenhower was showing continuity with American foreign policy since the Monroe Doctrine. Such ideological purity must be maintained, regardless of the suffering it caused.

Similarly, the hollowness of Eisenhower's anti-Communist crusade was made obvious by events in Hungary in

October and November of 1956. Egged on by American broadcasts on Radio Free Europe, the Hungarians rebelled against the Soviets and succeeded in driving them out. The Soviets, after a short while, counter-attacked in force, and crushed the revolt. Eisenhower refused to send any aid, ostensibly for fear of igniting a nuclear conflict. When Franco offered to send Spanish troops to assist the resistance, if the US would provide air transport, Ike refused. As eleven years earlier he had turned over Russians and Eastern Europeans to Stalin, so did he do again.

The cynical might be forgiven for suspecting that the real end in all of this was not the defeat of Communism, but simply maintenance of the Cold War, which had made both war-time prosperity and government control carry over.

THE ELECTION OF 1960

Whatever one might think of Kennedy's performance for the Houston ministers, it worked. He beat out Lyndon Johnson for the nomination of his Party, although taking on LBJ as Vice President.

On the Republican side, although the Conservatives (spearheaded by *National Review* and the Young Americans for Freedom) had made Arizona Senator Barry Goldwater a force to be reckoned with, Vice President Richard Nixon was easily nominated. He could be relied upon, if elected, to carry on Ike's policies.

The campaign saw the revival, for the last time, of the usual anti-Catholic calumnies (although JFK was the least deserving of such, as we have seen). He indulged, with Nixon, in the first ever presidential TV debates, which he won. Youthful and vigorous in appearance, he was married to the glamorous Jacqueline Bouvier; together they provided quite a contrast to the rather dowdy Eisenhowers. JFK was victorious in the November 8 election.

CAMELOT, THE HIPPIE ERA, AND THE GREAT SOCIETY

In the course of Eisenhower's farewell speech in 1961, he warned of the evils of the "military-industrial complex," which was odd, considering how much he had contributed to it. But JFK's inaugural speech, consisting as it did of marvelous and stirring phrases (including one pirated from Charles Evans Hughes—"Ask not what your country can do for you–ask what you can do for your country") captured the imagination of a generation coming of age.

Young and glamorous as the new first couple were (indeed, theirs would be the last formal inauguration–cutaway coats, top hats, and striped trousers–for another two decades), they seemed to epitomize what the nation's youth were looking for: a challenge to build a better world, and an attempt to transcend the mundane and dull culture in which they had been brought up. It was the age of Dr. Tom Dooley, the young Irish Catholic doctor whose work in setting up a hospital in Laos similarly caught the youthful imagination. On March 1, President Kennedy established the Peace Corps, which would send young American volunteers to various developing countries.

There is, because of the way the Kennedy administration ended, a sort of collective loss of memory which has descended over it. Because of the glamour, the high hopes, and the general atmosphere, it is remembered as "Camelot." The Civil Rights movement grew in strength and visibility, and young Americans dedicated themselves to various ways of improving things.

But in reality, JFK was not a very successful President. Only about 44% of the legislation he presented to Congress was passed. In foreign affairs, from the Bay of Pigs fiasco, to the Cuban Missile Crisis, to the escalation of American involvement in Vietnam, most of his foreign policy moves were less than helpful. To end the Missile Crisis, he had to withdraw our projectiles from Turkey. He persevered over the Berlin Blockade, thus leading to his famous "Ich bin ein Berliner" speech (intended no doubt to show his solidarity with the people of that beleaguered city, but actually proclaiming by this German phrase that he was a sort of jelly-filled doughnut). In Vietnam, the Catholic President Ngo Dinh Diem was assassinated in a coup, rumored by many to have been ordered by the US. If true, it was ironic, because a few weeks later, on November 22, Kennedy was assassinated in Dallas.

There have of course been all sorts of tales about the death of Kennedy. If it truly was some sort of conspiracy, it would have had to have been so large and powerful that detection is extremely unlikely. If there was none, then there is of course nothing to detect. However, it is highly doubtful that we shall ever know the truth. What is certain is that many of the young whose idealism had been inspired by JFK saw in his demise the death also of their hopes for decent change within the system.

Johnson and the Great Society

The new President was much more at home with Congress than Kennedy had been. Much that had been purely conceptual under JFK leapt to life under LBJ. On January 23, 1964, the Twenty-fourth amendment to the Constitution was approved, forbidding poll or other taxes to qualify voters. While obviously intended as a blow against Jim Crow, it had the effect of destroying a major element of the American voting process, which had been believed in by many of the Founding Fathers as essential to an intelligent electorate.

On March 16, Johnson addressed Congress and called for a "war on poverty." This would include formation of the Job Corps, and similar measures.

Meanwhile, the Civil Rights issue was heating up. After a 75-day long filibuster by Southern Senators, debate over the Civil Rights Bill of 1964 was cut off, and the measure passed. It banned racial discrimination in voting, education, public places, employment, and all federally aided programs. Its passage was the signal for hundreds of young white college students, the so-called "Freedom Riders," to bus down to Mississippi in order to register black voters. The Klan reacted predictably with floggings, terror, and in a few cases, murder. At the same time the "long hot summer" saw race riots rage in New York, New Jersey, Chicago, and Philadelphia.

The summer also saw the nominations for the Presidential elections. Johnson easily won his Party's; in the Republican Party, Goldwater triumphed over the liberal Nelson Rockefeller. From the beginning, Goldwater was the victim of a smear campaign until then unequaled in American electoral history. The result was predictable: November 3 saw a landslide for Johnson.

LBJ's own term began well enough. It did not end that way. In a speech given at the University of Michigan on May 22, 1964, he outlined his view of the "Great Society:"

> The Great Society rests on abundance and liberty for all. It demands an end to poverty and racial injustice, to which we are totally committed in our time. But that is just the beginning. The Great Society is a place where every child can find knowledge to enrich his mind and to enlarge his talents. It is a place where leisure is a welcome chance to build and reflect, not a feared cause of boredom and restlessness. It is a place where the city of man serves not only the needs of the body and the de-

mands of commerce but the desire for beauty and the
hunger for community.

It is a place where man can renew contact with nature. It is a place which honors creation for its own sake
and for what it adds to the understanding of the race. It
is a place where men are more concerned with the qual-
ity of their goals than the quantity of their goods. But,
most of all, the Great Society is not a safe harbor, a rest-
ing place, a final objective, a finished work; it is a challenge constantly renewed, beckoning us toward a destiny
where the meaning of our lives matches the marvelous
products of our labor.

In a word, what he offered was utopia. For a generation
looking for more than mere money, they were attractive words
indeed. But the Civil Rights movement seemed to lose mo-
mentum as riots broke out in ever more cities. After the
Gulf of Tonkin resolution planted us squarely in the Vietnam war, America's homes were able to watch it every night
on television. As it wore on, seemingly without point or end
in sight, it came to sum up for many all that was rotten with
the system which they had inherited.

College campuses from about 1965 became hotbeds of
political radicalism. The war—and the system—were against
Communism, weren't they? Then that is what many of its
opponents would embrace. Hence new Marxist groups like
the Students for a Democratic Society mushroomed. Together
with the ideas of the Beats, new forms of rock-n-roll spurred
by the arrival of the Beatles in 1964, the Eastern philoso-
phies like Zen championed by such as *Alan Watts*, and hal-
lucinogenic drugs popularized by *Timothy Leary*, this heady
brew produced the Counter Culture, or as its adherents came
to be known, the Hippies.

Casting off the gray and dark suits and short haircuts of
the '50's, Hippy men wore colorful clothes and long hair;

their "chicks" wore similarly unconventional attire. A whole new idiom of language, art and the like developed. Standards went out the window in dress, in manners, and much else.

Much of this was simply nonsense, but some was not. Putting to one side the drugs, free love, and crazed politics, what are we left with? A realization on the part of many of the Hippies that there really was something deeply wrong with America. For Theodore Roszak in his 1969 *The Making of a Counter Culture*, the movement at its best was an attempt to break through the arid, dry machine-age and Calvinist culture of the time, which he called the Technocracy:

> Understood...as the mature product of technological progress and the scientific ethos, the technocracy easily eludes all traditional political categories. Indeed, it is a characteristic of the technocracy to render itself ideologically invisible. Its assumptions about reality and its values become as unobtrusively persuasive as the air we breathe. While political argument continues within and between the capitalist and collectivist societies of the world, the technocracy increases and consolidates its power in both as a trans-political phenomenon following the dictates of industrial efficiency, rationality, and necessity (p.8).

For Roszak, much of what was valuable in the Counter Culture was simply a spiritual (if unguided) rejection of the technocracy. Some support might be garnered for his view when one considers the popularity among the Hippies of a perhaps unlikely book: a trilogy called *The Lord of the Rings*, written by a scholarly Oxford don named *J.R.R. Tolkien*.

Placed in an alternative world called Middle Earth, Tolkien's fantasy about dwarves, hobbits, elves, and the like pitted against the evil dark lord, Sauron, soon became a best

seller. It was not just that Tolkien's Middle Earth was magical
and pastoral; for one reason or another it seemed to answer
some of the deepest yearnings of the young. Peter S. Beagle
wrote for many of these in 1973, when he stated:

> I've never thought it an accident that Tolkien's works
> waited more than ten years to explode into popularity
> overnight. The Sixties were no fouler than the Fifties—
> they merely reaped the Fifties' foul harvest—but they were
> the years when millions of people grew aware that the
> industrial society had become paradoxically unlivable,
> incalculably immoral, and ultimately deadly. In terms of
> passwords, the Sixties were the time when the word
> progress lost its ancient holiness, and escape stopped be-
> ing comically obscene. The impulse is being called reac-
> tionary now, but lovers of Middle-earth want to go there.
> I would, like a shot.
>
> For in the end it is Middle-earth and its dwellers that
> we love, not Tolkien's considerable gifts in showing it to
> us. I said once that the world he charts was there long
> before him, and I still believe it. He is a great enough
> magician to tap our most common nightmares, day-
> dreams, and twilight fancies, but he never invented them
> either: he found them a place to live, a green alternative
> to each day's madness here in a poisoned world.

It is instructive to examine the opinions of JRRT himself
in regard to the topics we have been discussing. A man of
extremely conservative tastes and views, he nevertheless wrote:

> There are, of course, various elements in the present
> situation, which are confused, though in fact distinct (as
> indeed in the behavior of modern youth, part of which is
> inspired by admirable motives such as anti-regimenta-
> tion, and anti-drabness, a sort of romantic longing for
> "cavaliers," and not necessarily allied to the drugs or cults
> of fainéance and filth) [*Collected Letters*, p.393].

All of which having been said, what really was the secret of Tolkien's work's attraction to a generation raised on the dregs of Puritanism? Where was the magic? He wrote it down himself in another letter:

> I think I know exactly what you mean by the order of Grace; and of course by your references to Our Lady, upon which all my own small perception of beauty both in majesty and simplicity is founded. *The Lord of the Rings* is of course a fundamentally religious and Catholic work; unconsciously so at first, but consciously in the revision (p.172).

> ...I am a Christian (which can be deduced from my stories) and in fact a Roman Catholic. The latter "fact" perhaps cannot be deduced; though one critic (by letter) asserted that the invocations of Elbereth, and the character of Galadriel as directly described (or through the words of Gimli and Sam) were clearly related to devotion to Mary. Another saw in waybread (lembas)=viaticum and the reference to its feeding the *will* (vol. III, p.213) and being more potent when fasting, a derivation from Eucharist. (That is, far greater things may color the mind in dealing with the lesser things of a fairy story) [p.288].

Which brings one back to the question broached with the Beats. We see that, in veiled form, via Tolkien, the Hippies may have found what actually are elements of Catholicism compelling indeed, in the face of the materialism and drabness with which they were brought up. Why then did they not flock to the Faith, as so many Romantics had in their time?

The answer is that by that time the Church in America had conformed even in externals to the Americanist ethos, as to a degree, the Church Universal had done. We must now examine those circumstances.

VATICAN II AND THE
CATHOLIC REVOLUTION

With the accession of John XXIII, Church history entered its present phase. For better or worse, John XXIII is generally considered the author of the tide of change which has dominated Church affairs in our time.

Out of the blue, this Pope called a Council to no apparent end, then died in the middle of it. This allowed the Council Fathers (more particularly their "expert" assistants or *periti*) to do as they pleased. His changes in the Mass, small as they were, gave added impetus to liturgical vandals. Breaking with the anti-Communist stance of Pius XII, John began immediately sending out feelers to Moscow; in return for the presence of Russian and other Slavic Orthodox observers at his Council, he pledged that Communism would not be condemned there. Kruschev's son-in-law, an editor of *Pravda*, was received at the Vatican, and John XXIII received the Balzan Peace Prize, awarded by a Swiss-based Communist front organization.

There, at any rate, is one side of John XXIII. But justice compels us to look at another. On 22 February 1962, the Pope ordered published an Apostolic Constitution, that is, a communication of general authority, a most solemn document. Called *Veterum Sapientia*, it dealt with the use of Latin in the Church. In it, the Pope speaks of the value and importance of Latin. It is part of the Church's heritage, and further has great cultural and religious value. Latin is universal, immutable, and non-vernacular. In regard to this last he says: "..the Catholic Church has a dignity far surpassing that of every merely human society, for it was founded by Christ the Lord. It is altogether fitting, therefore, that the language it uses should be noble and majestic, and *non-vernacular*" (emphasis his; Cap.9). He then goes on to expound its educational value, following which he states the Church's official policy with regard to Latin:

> ...We also, impelled by the weightiest of reasons...are fully determined to restore this language to its position of honor and to do all We can to promote its study and use. The employment of Latin has recently been contested in some quarters, and many are asking what the mind of the Apostolic See is in this matter. We have therefore decided to issue the timely directives contained in this document, so as to ensure that the ancient and uninterrupted use of Latin be maintained and, where necessary, restored. (Cap.13).

The second section contains detailed instruction on Latin (and Greek) in clerical education. Theology and Philosophy are to be taught in Latin, and seminary professors unable to use it are to be gradually replaced. This is "Our Will."

Within the last decade, though, the last scrap of the language disappeared from the Mass. In the orgy of destruction which took place after the Council, every innovation, regardless of how cruel or absurd it was, was cloaked with a pious invocation of "Good Pope John."

There is too to be considered John's praiseworthy devotions to the Holy Ghost and the Precious Blood. He added "Blessed be the Holy Ghost, the Paraclete," and "Blessed be the Precious Blood of Jesus" to the Divine Praises at the end of Benediction. Further, he augmented the five approved-for-public-use litanies with that of the Precious Blood. But after his death, this devotion was even dropped from the calendar, supposedly to be subsumed under Corpus Christi; as with the Latin, his wishes meant little to those who came after. As Mark Antony said, "The evil that men do lives after them; the good is oft interred with their bones." So it was with Caesar, so, alas, with Pope John, of that name the Twenty-Third.

In 1960, just after John XXIII called for Vatican II, Dr. Hubert Jedin, Vatican archivist and historian of Trent, wrote an historical survey entitled *Ecumenical Councils in the Catholic Church*. To a degree, it was an attempt to explain the Councils to intelligent Catholic laymen. In the light of what actually transpired at Vatican II, it is interesting to quote his penultimate paragraph:

> It has always been the highest duty of a council to assure the proclamation of the faith by delimitating the Catholic doctrine from contemporary errors. There have been councils which issued no disciplinary canons, but none at which some error was not rejected, or some heretic excluded from the community of the faithful. No error of our time is more fraught with greater possibilities of evil than the atheistic doctrines of communism with their caricature of the ideal of human dignity which they actually seek to destroy, and no truth of the faith is in greater need of definition than the concept of the Church.

So thought Dr. Jedin. James Francis Cardinal McIntyre, Archbishop of Los Angeles, went to Vatican II hoping to get a definition on Limbo. But Vatican II was a Council unlike any other in the history of the Church. Speaking in Santiago, Chile, on 13 July 1988, Josef Cardinal Ratzinger, head of the Congregation for the Doctrine of the Faith characterized it in the following way:

> Vatican II is not seen as part of the living tradition of the Church, but as the end of the Tradition, as an annihilation of the past from which the directions to begin a new path are to be taken. The truth is that the Council itself defined no dogma and expressly wished to speak on a more modest level, merely as a pastoral Council. Despite this many interpret the present Council as if it were almost the superdogma that renders all the rest less important. (*30 Days*, June 1989, p.3).

Nor was this mere hindsight. John Cardinal Heenan, one of the participants at the Council, wrote in his 1966 work, *Council and Clergy*: "It deliberately limited its own objectives. There were to be no specific definitions. Its purpose from the first was pastoral renewal within the Church and a fresh approach to those outside."

All the other Councils of the Church met to define, to punish, and to correct. Since this was not to be the case with Vatican II, various of the Council Fathers asked for a decision on the theological status of the Council documents. The reply ? The Theological Commission of the Council replied on March 6, 1964 that "In view of the conciliar practice and pastoral purpose of the Council, this sacred Synod defines as binding on the Church only those matters of faith and morals which it has expressly put forward as such" (Flannery, O.P., Austin, ed., *Vatican Collection*, I, p.423). Paul VI had this declaration read to the Fathers as they prepared to vote on the Constitution on the Church, *Lumen Gentium*. In his General Audience of 12 January, 1966, the Pontiff declared that "in view of the pastoral nature of the Council, it avoided any extraordinary statements of dogmas endowed with the note of infallibility." In his closing speech at the Council, he had already remarked that "the Magisterium of the Church...did not wish to proclaim an extraordinary dogmatic sentence." Writing in the *Tablet*, March 2, 1968, p.199, Bishop B.C. Butler said very clearly: "There is no single proposition of Vatican II—except when quoting previous infallible definitions—which is in itself infallible."

All of this is important to realize. The sort of mentality which was a strong minority at Vatican I, was slapped on the wrist by Leo XIII, dove for cover under St. Pius X, was slightly relieved by Benedict XV, and successively liberated and wrist-slapped again by Pius XII, emerged as dominant at the Council. To understand the skullduggery that went on, your editors recommend *The Rhine Flows into the Tiber* by Fr. Ralph Wiltgen, SVD, *Pope John's Council*, by Michael Davies, and *Iota Unum* by Romano Amerio. We are more concerned here with results than process.

But if this was indeed a purely "pastoral" Council, would it not address Communism ? Instead:

> It may...puzzle some future students of late-twenti-eth century affairs when, seeking to understand how more than 2,000 Church leaders in the late 20th Century viewed the phenomenon of communism, they discover that the word "communism" is not even mentioned. Other significant–and not-so-significant–contemporary phenomena are discussed in the Council documents: the mass media, the problem of over-population, tax evasion, the need to follow basic practices of good hygiene, even the problem of reckless driving. How can one explain the mysterious absence from the Council's documents of the word "communism," a term of such importance for 20th century man–or at least for the two billion individuals who live under communist regimes? (Tommaso Ricci, *30 Days*, Sept. 1989, pp.58-9).

This statement was made in the context of a most illuminating article describing the attempt of 454 Council Fathers from 86 countries, to include an amendment to the Constitution *Gaudium et Spes*, "on the Church in the Modern World." The article includes the text of the amendment, which condemns Communism in strongest terms as "intrinsically perverse." It was brought up by these Fathers just prior to the end of the Council precisely because the set agenda provided did not even mention Communism. Unsurprisingly, this intervention was "misplaced" by French Bishop Achille Glorieux (secretary of the sub-commission for the revision of *Gaudium et Spes*) until it was too late to act upon. Ricci concludes:

Was the Council ever really free to decide on this point? This is what some contend. They argue that Glorieux's "forgetfulness" was intentional and was meant to avoid a "dangerous" vote in the Council hall. And why was it absolutely necessary that the Council not mention communism at all? Had a promise been made to someone?

A promise had been made. In return for the presence of Russian Orthodox observers at the Council, the Holy See agreed not to condemn Communism.

If it was not doctrinal, and if it did not deal with the then greatest pastoral problem facing the Church, what was the point of Vatican II? It was certainly the intention of a group of bishops and *periti* to alter the Church into a new religion. It should surprise no one that the two most influential clerics at the Council were the Modernist Karl Rahner, S.J., and the Americanist John Courtney Murray, S. J. As Fr. Wiltgen informs us, Conservative bishops and *periti*, in order to obtain an orthodox presentation in the documents, often had to compromise with Rahner and his followers and allow ambiguous phrasing (capable of an orthodox and/or heterodox interpretation) in disputed passages. Some, even of cardinalatial rank, warned Paul VI that the liberals planned to interpret *Lumen Gentium* in a liberal way after the Council:

> But the Pope still took no action because of his great faith in the Theological Commission. Then one of the extreme liberals made the mistake of referring, in writing, to some of these ambiguous passages, and indicating how they would be interpreted after the Council. This paper fell into the hands of the aforesaid group of cardinals and superiors general, whose representative took it to the Pope. Pope Paul, realizing finally that he had been deceived, broke down and wept. What was the remedy? Since the rest of the schema did not make any posi-

tively false assertion, but merely used ambiguous terms, the ambiguity could be clarified by joining to the text a carefully phrased explanation. This was the origin of the Preliminary Explanatory Note appended to the schema (Wiltgen, *op. cit.*, p.232).

Similar things were done with the other documents. In *Dignitatis Humanae,* the Declaration on Religious Liberty, for instance, whose primary author was John Courtney Murray, S.J., we see a direct refutation of the *Syllabus.* Among the propositions condemned therein are:

> 15. Every man is free to embrace and profess that religion which he, led by the light of reason, thinks to be the true religion.

> 16. In the worship of any religion whatever, men can find the way to eternal salvation, and can attain eternal salvation.

> 77. In this age of ours it is no longer expedient that the Catholic religion should be the only religion of the state, to the exclusion of all other cults whatsoever.

To this, *Dignitatis Humanae* answers, "the right to religious freedom is based on the very dignity of the human person as known through the revealed word of God and by reason itself" (Flannery, *op. cit.*, I, 800). The declaration prattles on and on, making hair-splitting distinctions, and explicitly rejecting prior teaching. It concludes by saying:

> It is clear that with the passage of time all nations are coming into a closer unity, men of different cultures and religions are being bound together by closer links, and there is a growing awareness of individual responsibility. Consequently, to establish and strengthen peaceful relations and harmony in the human race, religious freedom must be given effective constitutional protection everywhere and that highest of man's rights and duties—to lead

a religious life with freedom in society—must be respected. (Flannery, *op. cit.*, I, 812).

Contrast this, dear reader, with these words of Leo XIII in *Immortale Dei*, (Cap.32):

> ...the State is acting against the laws and dictates of nature whenever it permits the license of opinion and of action to lead minds astray from truth and souls away from the practice of virtue.

The Declaration rightly reiterated the traditional Church teaching that no one must be forced into the Church against his will. But it went on beyond that to say that no restrictions must be put on the individual's practice of a non-Catholic religion (such as forbidding proseletyzing, employment of Catholic servants, public demonstrations, etc.). Completely absent was any concept of truth versus error—there was only the "search for truth in freedom."

It is not only Conservatives who have problems with Council documents. No, certain documents are problematic for the Liberals. A typical example is *Sacrosanctum Concilium*, the decree on the liturgy. The document orders non-specific revision of the liturgy, laying down ambiguous directions: "36. (1) The use of the Latin language, with due respect to the particular law, is to be preserved in the Latin rites. (2) But since the use of the vernacular, whether in the Mass, the administration of the sacraments, or in other parts of the liturgy, may frequently be of great advantage to the people, a wider use may be made of it." So; the Latin is to be preserved? With due respect to particular law? Which law? Where, how, and when? As for the vernacular, how could it be of great advantage to the people? The average Catholic in 1963 no more wanted the vernacular in the Mass then he wanted dancers in it. Post-Conciliar experience has shown

that it has failed to retain large numbers of Catholics, nor
has it recruited new ones. But how did the Church observe
the injunction that the Latin was to be preserved? We shall
let Fr. Flannery speak himself:

> ...restrictions on the use of the vernacular were pro-
> gressively lifted in the face of representations by hierar-
> chies from all over the world, until by 1971 the use of
> the vernacular in public Masses was left entirely to the
> judgment of episcopal conferences, to the judgment of
> individual priests for public Masses, and of the ordinary
> for divine office in private, in common, or in choir.
>
> Strangely enough, the ruling that translations of the
> breviary had to carry the Latin text as well was not for-
> mally revoked, but it was no longer applied after a while.
> (Flannery, *op. cit.*, I, 39).

So it was with Council orders on retention of Gregorian
Chant and polyphony at Mass, and of the teaching of Latin
in seminaries. Because the plain fact of the matter was that
the staff of most episcopal conferences, the Roman bodies
"implementing" the Conciliar decrees, many of the individual
bishops, and countless theologians, etc., all had a vested interest in transforming Catholicism into something alien. The
result was a burst of legislation which, apparently issued or
tolerated by the highest offices in the Church, effectively
made the Church unrecognizable in less than a decade.

But where does that leave the Council itself? As was said
of the Protestant Revolt, "what was good in it was not new,
and what was new was not good." Richard O'Connor, writing in the *Homiletic and Pastoral Review* (July 1981, pp.5-6)
put it thusly:

> What is more important is to make clear the *kind* of
> assent demanded of the faithful...What this means, as
> Pope John Paul II never tires of emphasizing when refer-

ring to Vatican II, is that it is to be interpreted in the light of Tradition, of other Councils, and Papal Encyclicals; and, where found to be in conflict with these, disregarded."

"It is all well and good," you may say, "to ignore Vatican II, and concentrate on the immemorial teachings and devotions of the Church. But Catholic life is not just reading the Fathers and saying the rosary in front of the family Sacred Heart picture. It is attending a parish, sending your children to school, and performing your civic duties in accord with Church teaching. You say that this is next to impossible outside the declining numbers of 'conservative' parishes, and impossible even there if you want the practices of the immemorial Church *in toto*. What to do?"

Well, as one might imagine, the first reaction would be to appeal to the Pope. Paul VI was not unaware that things were out of control at the Council. He took decisive action there: he wept. Then he added codicils that were ignored.

In response to all the horrible things happening throughout the universal Church, the Pope responded firmly in various well reported 1972 statements:

> By means of some fissure the smoke of Satan has entered the temple of God....One no longer trusts the Church....It was believed that after the Council there would be a day of sunshine in the history of the Church....There came instead a day of clouds, storms, and darkness, of search and uncertainty...through an adverse power; his name is the devil....Perhaps the Lord has called me not to govern and save the Church, but to suffer for her, and to make it clear that he and no one else, guides and saves her.

In the face of such unparalleled confusion in the Church, such a declaration could be taken as an effective abdication. His Holiness would do nothing to stem the tide, would not

attempt to be the Rock of the Church, but would be terribly
upset by it all. There is a Latin maxim: "what is permissible
to Jove, is not permissible to an ox." By the same token,
what is permissible to an ox, is not permissible to Jove.

Many have compared Paul VI to Hamlet; for he acqui-
esced to practically anything, no matter how dreadful. Oh,
he might put up a token defense, as against Communion in
the hand in *Memoriale Domini*. But if enough bishops backed
a measure, he generally gave in. He did at least repeat the
Church's teaching on contraception in *Humanae Vitae* against
much (including episcopal) opposition in 1968. What could
we say of him? In his day, it seemed (on a practical basis) that
there was no one in charge at the Vatican at all. The local
hierarchies did just as they pleased, only invoking Papal authority when useful in quashing orthodox resistance to them;
in response, droves of Catholics in the developed nations
either left or simply dropped out. Hamlet? This Pontificate
was rather reminiscent of Chorus' last speech in *Henry V*:

> Henry the Sixth, in infant bands crown'd king
> Of France and England, did this king succeed;
> Whose state so many had the managing
> That they lost France and made his England bleed.

In the United States, soon after the Council, various
voices were raised in protest against the changes which had
occurred. Most notable, perhaps, was *Triumph* magazine.
Published by Brent Bozell, it featured such writers as Molnar
and Wilhelmsen; associated with it also were *John Wisner*,
Gary Potter, and *Farley Clinton*, to name a few. Originally
closely connected with Buckley (Bozell's brother-in-law) and
the *National Review*, *Triumph* came more and more to repre-
sent an integral Catholic point of view, and so its staff began
to see in "Conservatism" simply the right wing of the national liberalism. (Meanwhile, Buckley has progressively

cozied himself up to the Eastern Liberal Establishment.)

There were likewise American priests who, at an early date, foresaw the problems which were about to fall on the unsuspecting heads of Catholic America.

But all of these prophetic voices were considered eccentric by mainstream Catholics. They preferred to do as they were told; this appeared to be simply imitating Methodists. Given all of this, when the youth of America began to look beyond the now-discredited old-style version of Americanism for answers, all they could see in Catholicism was more of the same. This was a bitterly ironic recognition of the fact that the accomodationists had "succeeded" only too well in achieving their goal: making a compartmental, puritanical, jingoistic caricature of the genuine Catholic religion, so as to get a piece of the affluent American Pie. Thus, it was tainted with the same reputation for hypocrisy that post-World War II American society deservedly came in for as a whole (disregarding momentarily the wayward motives of the protesters).

This judgment was all but confirmed with Vatican II, which, in surrendering to the modern world, appeared to give the lie to everything that the Catholic religion taught these youths before that disastrous Council! In such conditions, there was virtually no chance that the Truth would reach those who most desperately needed it of all. Even *if* the youth would listen, who was now going to give it to them, when the clergy and religious were too busy discarding whatever was still good about pre-Vatican II Catholicism?

THE SPACE PROGRAM

Lyndon Johnson, his administration rendered ineffective by national unrest, decided not to run again. In the election of 1968, his place was taken by his Vice President, Hubert Humphrey. Humphrey, however lost to the Republican, Richard Nixon. Thus, eight years after his defeat by JFK, Nixon found himself President-elect of a very different nation.

During all the political and social turmoil, one thing had gone forward: the nation's Space Program. In reaction to the Soviet's 1957-58 launch of history's first artificial satellites (under the Sputnik project, with all the implications such an event would have for the Cold War), the National Aeronautics and Space Administration (NASA) had presided over the launching of manned spaceships.

First of these was the Mercury series, comprising a one-man capsule designed to revolve around the earth. On February 20, 1962, John Glenn successfully completed orbit in outer space.

Three years later, the first manned Gemini capsule, with two crew members, took its place on March 23, 1965. Before the last Gemini was launched on November 11, 1966, astronauts had space-walked. Now the great race to put a man on the moon, announced by President Kennedy, was on in earnest.

There were a number of mishaps with the so-called Apollo project. But at last, on July 20, 1969, Neil Armstrong set foot on the moon. He did not claim it for the United States, since this country had signed an Outer Space convention under U.N. auspices resigning all territory outside the atmosphere. But a great dream had been accomplished, a great triumph for American technology. As long as man had existed, he had dreamt of the moon; now he had walked there.

If the science fiction movies of the 1950's had not precisely predicted the actual event, they had helped create a climate in which the public would support the measure. Were heaven to be cut off from them as myth, they would settle for space.

AFTERWORD

So at last we have come to the end of our tale. It is not really the end of course, because history, American or otherwise, can have no end until the time for the Last Judgment. But we leave off at the utmost triumph of the American idea: man's conquest of the moon.

What things we should dwell upon were we to continue! The end of the war in Vietnam, and the agony of Watergate; the Reagan "revolution" and the fall of Communism; the legalization of abortion and homosexuality, and continued decay of Church and State, as a direct consequence of this triumph of the American ideal. But in these we enter into the realm of current events.

What is to be made of the tapestry which has gone before? What patterns can be discerned? At times we have made some comment upon them in the course of this history, but having come to the end, let us look at them a little more closely.

American history is the tale of two simultaneous developments: the gradual weeding out of the practices and beliefs of old Christendom on the one hand, and their replacement with an ever more elaborate ethos which promised a purely secular salvation. In place of the organic national life offered by the first, America received, as it were, a simulacrum of nationhood, the artificiality of which was effectively concealed by economic prosperity.

The Puritan Fathers came here originally to establish a commonwealth free of "Papist" influences. Despite this, they were men of a formerly Catholic culture, and sketched out for their heretical conventicles a place in society roughly equivalent to that of the Church in fully-Catholic societies. A whisper of this remains in the location of Congregational and/or Unitarian churches of the village commons of New England, echoing faintly the setting of plazas throughout Europe and Latin America.

When the Enlightenment and its accompanying Masonry hit these shores, they spread most rapidly among the sons of the Puritans, gradually destroying the place even of the Bible in their minds, but leaving their Calvinist attitudes and anti-Catholicism intact. This odd mixture became the intellectually dominant force in the 13 colonies. Under its influence the ruling circles here joined forces with their Whig equivalents in England, and destroyed in America the second most important institution of Christendom, the Monarchy.

After the Revolution, "Americanism" became a religion of its own. At first, it was a self-contradictory combination of liberal and Christian elements: an obsessive rhetoric of individual freedom and equality (and, note well, *not* along the lines of the New Testament!) was coupled with notions of "God, Family, and Country," alongside certain natural virtues—even if these notions were tainted with Calvinism. In its name, and despite its original orientation to "federalism," that third key element of Christendom, local liberties (called "subsidiarity" by the Popes, and "States' Rights" in this country) was at first gradually and then forcefully put an end to. One after another, French and Spanish influences within our boundaries were conquered and then assimilated. The unholy trinity of Noah Webster, Horace Mann, and finally John Dewey, refashioned American education from its original aim to being purely a tool of social engineering.

Through it, generations of immigrants from abroad were systematically "cleansed" of their cultures, and made loyal adherents of the Americanist faith.

Interior unity achieved, and financial success secured, the Americanist religion traveled overseas, first to Latin America and thence to the world. In every case, the wealth and power of this nation were committed by her leadership to the destruction of any Catholic political power which remained. Thus did Spain and Austria-Hungary go under, and thus were innumerable gimcrack separation-of-Church-and-State republics ushered in throughout the globe. The rise of Communism permitted the installation of Americanist values under the guise of "freedom" in our allies' societies, even as Communism's fall has allowed the same in the former enemy nations. Pornography is, after all, one of our primary exports to such nations. Now, acceptance of contraception and abortion is a must for any struggling country to receive US aid.

Of the institutions of Christendom, the family is the one which has survived longest under the rule of an Americanism that systematically worked out its initial self-contradiction by gradually ridding itself of the accouterments of Christian culture. But having been first undermined via contraception and abortion, it is now the direct focus of attack, via such things as redefining child abuse and recognizing "domestic partnerships" as fully legitimate alternatives to marriage. In truth, all that remains now is the individual, the hero of old-time Americanist rhetoric, and supposedly still the focus of today's version of the religion.

But he will not be allowed to remain beyond the reach of the encroaching State for long. Through euthanasia, increased government monitoring of such "vices" as tobacco and alcohol, and of course the ever more thoroughly enforced expression of "politically correct" speech and behavior, the individual too must become increasingly the ward of an all-powerful government. In return, however, said individual will have access to ever more refined methods of entertainment. In a word, Aldous Huxley's *Brave New World* appears to be en route–this latter being, of course, the "Universal Republic" dreamed of by the Freemasonry of the Enlightenment.

Such is the state of affairs made by this inevitable purification of the Americanist religion into unalloyed liberalism, which needs an "inquisition" to protect its singular dogma: that outside the self, there is no reality, truth, ethics, or fulfillment. The message of 1990's society is all too clear; he who insists on objectivity, let him be anathema! And those who believe in this dogma will be, of course, useful and docile idiots where the New World Order is concerned. Satan knows his goats, and–deep down–they know him.

Over the past few centuries, then, first Church, then King, then local liberties, then family, and at last the individual have been disposed of. What has been the attitude of the Church, then?

When the Church enters a heathen land, it is usually her first interest to convert its people as quickly as she may. This includes baptizing whatever local customs may be compatible with Catholic teaching; the same is done with native institutions. The reason for this (and for the frequent martyrdoms of missionaries and converts which often result) are the glory of God and the salvation of souls. When a country becomes primarily or entirely Catholic, the public face of that nation changes; there emerges the Catholic State, which recognizes as its primary duty the assistance of the Church in her divine mission. Thus it was in old Europe; thus also (although not so well known) in Latin America; thus at last in those parts of Asia and Africa which were thoroughly evangelized.

But in the United States this pattern was in no wise followed. From the first, the Catholic community in the 13 colonies was a despised minority; its lay leadership by the time of the Revolution was committed to a policy of accommodation with the ruling classes, and its spiritual leadership purely to servicing the needs of those already Catholic. There could be no question of converting the nation.

Independence brought forth new opportunities. The rush of immigrants from abroad increased the numbers of American Catholics tremendously. The response of "native" Americans to this was to be found in such incidents as the Know-Nothing riots. "Nativism" of this sort, although re-erupting periodically, was not put to an end by the growth of Catholicism—quite the contrary. Such men as James Cardinal Gibbons assured Protestant Americans that the Church regarded the United States as perfect *in their current religious and political condition.* In a word, co-existence rather than conversion was the goal of American Catholicism. Any stirring on the part of the Catholic faithful in the direction of more integral Catholicity was sternly squelched by the hierarchy.

Although condemned by Leo XIII, Americanism in its form as a Catholic heresy became in the end the dominant belief in the Church in this country. When Modernism arose in Europe, it was brought over to this country, swiftly germinating in a soil well prepared for it. The efforts of our country overseas left America the dominant military, economic, political, cultural, and social force on the globe—which development was echoed in the Church. Vatican II signaled acceptance of Americanism by the leadership of the Church—particularly as regards Religious Freedom, Ecumenism, and Separation of Church and State. From the beginning, it would appear that Rome had not realized the danger Americanism posed—had not realized until it was too late.

Here we stand then, in the closing years of the 20th century. Many believe the role of the Church to be that of a mere spiritual cheerleader for the New World Order. Certainly, this would appear to be a legitimate extension of the role of the American Church under the headship of such as Cardinal Gibbons and Archbishop Ireland.

All of this having been said, American history appears much of the time as a chronicle of lost opportunities, of victories for the wrong side—in a word, as tragedy. But if tragedy it be, said tragedy is not a result of any especial evil in the American character, but of cowardice and dereliction on the part of the country's Catholics.

Where then, do we stand? In what does true patriotism consist for an orthodox Catholic American? How is he able to love the country of his birth, which has done so much to destroy his Faith at home and abroad, and which incarnates, so to speak, the principles of secularism to which he must ever be opposed?

The first is to identify in the country's history and present those strands which are most acceptable to the Faith—for in truth, there is much to love and admire in this country. In the settlements of the French and Spanish in the Southwest and the Mississippi and Great Lakes basins; in the towns founded by Catholic immigrants where some of their culture yet remains; and even in those regions such as the Appalachians and the rural South and New England where a bit of the once Catholic ethos of the British Isles survives; in these and other places, folk-lore and song provide what might one day be elements of a foundation for a truly Catholic culture. On many Indian reservations, one yet finds some of the spirit or at least artifacts of the missionaries, like Frs. Serra and De Smet. Every Catholic American should try to know something of the original settlers of the spot in this country where he lives, as well as of his own ancestors.

For in these United States, as we have seen, are settled

people from virtually every country in the world. In microcosm we can see the building blocks of that "one fair realm
of charity" which the hymn for the Feast of Christ the King
asks God to create by enfolding "all lands, all tribes." Despite the ever-grinding forces of assimilation, enough remains
of the cultures which settled here to offer some alternative to
the Americanist vision.

Building blocks, however, are not the finished product,
anymore than savage Germanic tribes and the decadent Roman Empire were themselves together Christendom. Then
as now, it required the vivifying force of the Faith to give
those stones life. What we have is in fact a half-life, as has
been said; whether we are to be Pinocchio or Frankenstein
depends on how and whether the life-giving sacraments are
applied to this nation—not as private practice, but as public
act.

We saw that Pius XI declared in his 1926 *Quas Primas*:
"When men once recognize, both in private and in public
life, that Christ is King, society will at last receive the great
blessings of real liberty, well-ordered discipline, peace and
harmony." The Pontiff goes on to describe what great blessings would result to individuals, families, nations, and the
world at large, were this done. But practically speaking, it
can only happen if this nation is converted. There is where
true patriotism is to be found for the American Catholic.
Such a one who blithely accepts the religious status quo in
America, as did Carroll, as did Gibbons, as did Spellman, is
no friend to his country, its peoples, or their liberty.

For what will happen if the United States are not converted? Either present trends will continue, or they will not.

If they do, and this nation will be the center of a world-
wide and despotic republic which will not only grind down
its subjects' humanity, but cause them to love their chains
and lose their souls. The unspeakable can become quite com-

fortable if dwelt with long enough. It might be hard to see a worse alternative.

Still, one might. The other possibility is that this technocracy in which we live will collapse of its own weight, its own sterility, its own lack-of-birth-rate. Then will the denizens of the Third World, stripped of Christian love, but well-educated in secular greed to envy the goods of the wealthier nations, rise up and drown them in blood. Or perhaps, beyond the calculations of our leaders, famine, plague, and natural disaster will shatter our fragile infrastructure. How then would our fellow-citizens deal with the great realities of fear and horror, unshielded by technology nor consoled by the religion which it replaced?

Nor let it be thought that political action alone or even primarily can save the Great Republic. One of our regular errors has been to think that Catholics allied with Protestants in order to win victory at the polls for this principle or against that abuse will affect much in the long run. These battles can be useful in the immediate; but they have tended to take our eyes off the main goal and only true solution for the country's ills: the conversion of America. The stories of Fr. Coughlin, Msgr. Ryan, and *The Catholic Worker* (to say nothing of today's Pro-Life Movement) should tell us something.

Mr. Paul Blanshard (with whom we met earlier), an avid hater of the Church, fully acquainted himself with her social teachings in order to show the difference between Catholicism and Americanism. He, of course, espoused the latter. Nevertheless, his contrasting the two religion's beliefs on important social issues is revealing:

> *Divorce:* The Catholic Church says: "The State has no right to grant divorces since it has no authority to annul a valid marriage." The federal and state governments dis-

agree. The American people now permit divorce in every state.

Marriage: The Church refuses to recognize marriages as valid when non-Catholic clergymen or public officials perform marriage ceremonies for Catholics. The people, through the United States government and state governments refuse to discriminate against marriages of Catholics by non-Catholic clergymen.

Birth Control: The Church says that all use of contraceptives by non-Catholics or Catholics is illegal under Church law. The people in all but two states of the United States permit doctors to give contraceptive advice to patients. [In 1967 the US Supreme Court abolished any and all restrictions on birth control].

Education: The Church teaches that Catholic schools should be supported by public (non-Catholic and Catholic) taxpayers and that priests should have the right to censor public school text books. The people have enacted both state and federal laws to make *direct* contributions to Catholic schools illegal, and nominally they reject Catholic censorship in public schools.

Sterilization: The people in twenty-seven states, permit some eugenic sterilization of certain insane, feeble-minded, and criminal citizens under certain specific safeguards. The Church says this is illegal and immoral, except as a specific penalty for crime.

Therapeutic abortion: The Church says that therapeutic abortion is murder even if it is absolutely necessary to save the life of a mother. The people in all states permit therapeutic abortion when it is indicated to save the life or health of a mother. [In 1973, the Supreme Court legalized abortion under all circumstances, under any pretext whatsoever. Mean old Church opposed this too!] (*American Freedom and Catholic Power*, p.22).

Obviously, Blanshard here identifies the mandate of the rulership with the will of the people; this identification has, through the history recounted, been shown to be false. But in the minds of many Americans, whatever their own views on these topics, the same identification is made.

Regardless, all of these topics strike at the very heart of a people; the non-Catholic view has prevailed, and the result has been the near-complete transformation of a Puritanical-Masonic regime into a purely inhuman one–and all in the name of freedom.

As recounted earlier, Blanshard declared that American Catholics had a hidden agenda to "subject" this nation to the Church's social teachings. We have seen the great outrage this brought about in US Catholic circles, and the resulting dispute between Frs. John Courtney Murray and Joseph C. Fenton regarding relations between Church and State. But Blanshard had outlined what he believed would become of the vaunted American Democracy, did the Catholics gain political power. This was a list of three amendments to the Constitution.

The first he called the "Christian Commonwealth Amendment:"

> 1. The United States [are] a Catholic Republic, and the Catholic Apostolic and Roman religion is the sole religion of the nation.
>
> 2. The authority of the Roman Catholic Church is the most exalted of all authorities; nor can it be looked upon as inferior to the power of the United States government, or in any manner dependent upon it, since the Catholic Church as such is a sovereign power.
>
> 3. Priests and members of religious orders of the Roman Catholic Church who violate the law are to be tried by an ecclesiastical court of the Roman Catholic Church, and may, only with the consent of the competent Catho-

lic authority, be tried by the courts of the United States or the states.

4. Apostate priests or those incurring the censure of the Roman Catholic Church cannot be employed in any teaching post or any office or employment in which they have immediate contact with the public.

5. Non-Catholic faiths are tolerated, but public ceremonies and manifestations other than those of the Roman Catholic religion will not be permitted.

6. The First Amendment to the Constitution of the United States is hereby repealed.

This shocker was to be followed up by the "Christian Education Amendment:"

1. American religious education belongs pre-eminently to the Roman Catholic Church, by means of a double title in the supernatural order, conferred exclusively upon her by God Himself.

2. The Roman Catholic Church has the inalienable right to supervise the entire education of her children in all educational institutions in the United States, public or private, not merely in regard to the religious instruction given in such institutions, but in regard to every other branch of learning and every regulation in so far as religion and morality are concerned.

3. Compulsory education in public schools exclusively shall be unlawful in any state of the union.

4. It shall be unlawful for any neutral or non-Catholic school to enroll any Catholic child without permission of the Church.

5. Since neutral schools are contrary to the fundamental principles of education, public schools in the United States are lawful only when both religious instruction and every other subject taught are permeated with Catholic piety.

6. The governments of the United States and of the States are permitted to operate their own schools for military and civic training without supervision by the Roman Catholic Church, provided they do not injure the rights of said Church, and provided that only the Roman Catholic Church shall have the power to impart religious instruction in such schools.

7. With due regard to special circumstances, co-education shall be unlawful in any educational institution in the United States whose students have attained the age of adolescence.

8. The governments of the United States and of the states shall encourage and assist the Roman Catholic Church by appropriate measures in the exercise of the Church's supreme mission as educator.

Then at last came the "Christian Family Amendment:"

1. The government of the United States, desirous of restoring to the institution of matrimony, which is the basis of the family, that dignity conformable to the traditions of its people, assigns as civil effects of the sacrament of matrimony all that is assigned to it by the Canon Law of the Roman Catholic Church.

2. No matrimonial contract in the United States that involves a Catholic can be valid unless it is in accordance with the Canon Law of the Roman Catholic Church.

3. Marriages of non-Catholics are subject to the civil authority of the state, but all civil laws that contradict the Canon Law of the Roman Catholic Church are hereby declared null and void.

4. All marriages are indissoluble, and the divorce of all persons is prohibited throughout the territory of the United States: provided that nothing herein shall affect the right of annulment and remarriage in accordance with the Canon Law of the Roman Catholic Church.

5. Attempted mixed marriages or unions between members of the Roman Catholic Church and non-Catholics are null and void, unless a special dispensation is obtained from the ecclesiastical authority of the Catholic Church.

6. Birth control, or any act that deliberately frustrates the natural power to generate life, is a crime.

7. Direct abortion is murder of the innocent even when performed through motives of misguided pity when the life of a mother is gravely imperiled.

8. Sterilization of any human being is prohibited except as an infliction of grave punishment under the authority of the government for a crime committed.

This supposed "Catholic Master Plan" for America received much criticism from Catholic and non-Catholic critics of Blanshard alike. But Blanshard rightly defended it, declaring (p.305):

> I remember a verse from Job which is appropriate at this moment: "If I justify myself, mine own mouth shall condemn me." That is meant for Catholic liberals whose temperature has been rising while they have been reading these three amendments. As most of my readers have doubtless guessed, there is not a single original word in my entire three Catholic amendments. They are mosaics of official Catholic doctrine. *Every concept, almost every line and phrase, has been plagiarized line by line from Catholic documents.* The most important phrases are derived from the highest documents [sic!] of Catholicism, the encyclicals of the Popes. The provisions on education come from Pius XI's *Christian Education of Youth*, and those on family life from his *Casti Connubii*, both of them accepted universally in the Catholic Church as the Bibles of present-day educational and family policy. A few provisions are taken directly from Canon Law, the recent laws of Catholic countries like Spain, and the 1929 Concordat between Mussolini and the Vatican, all of

which have been publicly approved by Catholic authorities. Only place-names and enabling clauses have been added to give the Papal principles local application. The sources are listed in the notes.

Needless to say, the principles contained in these "amendments" are inimical to everything most Americans hold dear. What Blanshard could not have realized was that not only were American Catholic Liberals sincere in their repudiation of them, their strength was such that in a mere decade and a half, they and their foreign allies would force the Church (even in Spain, Italy, and Ireland) to *de facto* acceptance of the American way. The authentic social teachings of the Church were presented by the governing circles of the Church as merely the opinions of certain Popes or else the much-attacked Roman Curia. Even so late as 1992, Bishop Mark J. Hurley, former ordinary of Santa Rosa, California, could write:

> These [the cases of Fr. Robert Drinan, pro-abortion Jesuit ex-Congressman; Fr. Charles Curran, former CUA dissenting moral theologian; and Archbishop Raymond Hunthausen of Seattle] and other incidents rightly caused legitimate concern in both Catholic and non-Catholic circles. The Roman Curia, notoriously uninstructed and untutored in things American, and hiding behind the anonymity of a Byzantine bureaucracy, continued to make mischief right into the 1990's to the despair of many bishops as well as others...

> The repressions, quiet censorship, removal from office, and other actions gave non-Catholics, in particular, grounds for concern as to where the Church stood on basic liberties, the American bishops to the contrary notwithstanding.

> Thanks in large part to the Roman curial actions over the years, two centuries to be exact, those who viewed

the American Catholics with distrust were not fighting
straw men. Thoughtful men and women asked fair questions; demagogues ran wild (*The Unholy Ghost*, p.52).

Despite the fact that today the Vatican would be much
more likely to discipline a theologian who upheld literally
Pius IX's *Syllabus of Errors* or Pius XI's *Quas Primas* and
Quadragesimo Anno, here Bishop Hurley identifies the Curia's
spasmodic efforts to address the most notorious attacks of
Catholic dogma and morals with everything anti-Catholics
hated in her social teachings. Obviously, so long as the American hierarchy are largely of such mind, the bones of Paul
Blanshard may rest as easily as his eternal reward permits.

Yet it is precisely the sort of measures Blanshard describes
which are required to save this nation from the twin threats
of dystopia and bloody anarchy which appear to await us.
Obviously, they are a bare minimum; but think on the benefits which would accrue! Were something like his Christian
Family Amendment passed, all the evils which have disrupted
the family and reduced the young folk of this country to
rootless and selfish eternal children would be alleviated. The
birthrate of the native-born would rise, thus saving us from
an eroding tax-base (with the threat of Social Security's collapse). If marriages were permanent, the evils and crime resulting from broken homes would be alleviated.

The educational amendment, banishing the spirit of
Webster, Mann, and Dewey from the classroom, would ac-
centuate improving conditions for America's children, and
so for her future. In place of what was social engineering and
has become often a physically dangerous day-care center for
adolescents, the classroom would become a place whose products would be able to think rationally, would have the academic and technical skills to compete in the job market (and
assist the nation in competing with foreign countries), and
would have the moral background necessary for a produc-

tive and happy adulthood.

Above all, the Commonwealth amendment would place this country in a position to receive the benefits promised by Pius XI in *Quas Primas* in terms of societal harmony and solidarity. It would further lay a foundation for a reorganization of the country's political and economic life along the lines of *Rerum Novarum, Quadragesimo Anno*, and the rest— in a word, the beginning of a truly just society.

But political action will not achieve this. No party, no political action committee for a major corporation, no lobbyist group, will push for such a program. Had the first Christian Emperor, Philip the Arabian, ordered the Roman Empire to become thoroughly Christian in every detail—in a word, to become Christendom—it would not have happened. Fiats from above did not create Christendom, although in time they could destroy it. Rather, the long work of missionaries—lay and religious—over many centuries, and the ever increasing and deeper Catholicism of succeeding generations did so. The Germanic warrior code became chivalry; classical philosophy and literature became Christian; the Roman patricians and barbarian chiefs became the European nobility; and so on.

In this same way must this country be converted. But to do so, we orthodox American Catholics must give up our habitual way of looking at our country and our place in it. To do less is an insult to God, and (seeing that the survival of this nation depends upon it) a form of treason.

To begin with, let us realize that we do not live in a Christian land. Though we may proudly think differently, our political factions and feuds (save where they directly concern Catholic interests or moral issues) are for the most part of no more moment than those of warring tribes in New Guinea. Our primary reason for being here is to show, by our actions, our desire to accept God's offer of eternal union

with Him according to the terms and conditions He laid out
(whereby, among other things, we will urge others to do likewise)—not to push for sound money or a clean environment
(although such activity—apart from short term gains for the
community—provide exposure to sympathetic people who
might be willing to listen to our religious message). Yet here
we must beware of the opposite thing happening; coopera-
tion with friendly non-Catholics in the political sphere must
not have the effect of legitimizing their religion for us. The
danger of the missionary "going native" is an ever present
one.

Yet we cannot really be missionaries unless we are integral Catholics ourselves. In part, this is a question of learning everything possible about the Faith: her dogmas, her history, and her practices. The English *Denzinger* and Dom
Prosper Guéranger's *The Liturgical Year*, as a bare minimum,
should be in every Catholic home. To the study of the Faith
should go the energy and interest that are often directed to
other, less important goals, such as the memorizing of sports
scores.

Beyond this, however, we have to actively reconquer our
own minds. Rather than accept what is given us on television or in the movies, we should try to fill our heads with
such things as the Catholic legends and tales of valor, like
the stories of King Arthur and Charlemagne. The Catholic-
inspired folk customs of song, cookery, and celebration native either to our ancestors or the region we live in (or both)
should determine the atmosphere of our homes, in addition
to the presence of statues and paintings of the saints. Let us
keep Advent until Christmas Eve, keep Christmas until the
Epiphany, feast during Carnival, and fast during Lent. In a
word, to the degree that we can, we need to make our own
homes foretastes of the America that ought to be.

But it is not enough to do this for ourselves. Practically

speaking, our non- and fallen-away Catholic friends and rela-
tives are the obvious field for us to work in. Once we begin
to think of these people not as folk of whom we are fond yet
who are spiritually secure, but as souls who need the light of
Faith whom (in all likelihood) we may be the only ones capable of bringing it to, all sorts of methods of doing this will
suggest themselves.

Be ready to speak about and defend the Faith under any
and all circumstances, while yet avoiding the "sledgeham-
mer" approach especially with those whose intellectual state
does not permit them to think clearly about religion—or anything else, for that matter. With such people, it is *essential*
that they get back in touch with natural reality, before they
are fit for being presented with the grand realities of the true
religion. When your co-workers are only too happy to talk
about their children's bar mitzvahs and Sunday schools, be
sure to speak of your own children's catechism classes and
Christmas pageants.

It is not an easy task; in truth, if we all do our part, the
likelihood is that one day Catholics in this country will be
martyred. It is always the case in lands where the Faithful do
their job. Martyrdom was presented to us by the Know Noth-
ings and the Nativists; our response was to burn incense on
the altars of the gods. We have profited materially, but lost
our souls thereby.

When our fathers converted the Empire, through the
grace of God they brought off a miracle. We do not think of
it that way, but through their work, pagan Gaul and its pagan Frank invaders became France, the oldest daughter of
the Church; the wreck of Roman Britain, seized by the blood-
thirsty Saxons, became England, Our Lady's Dowry; pagan
Spain saw after her conversion her Visigothic invaders embrace the Faith, and when Goth and Spaniard were subju-
gated by the Moors that Faith sustained them through eight

centuries of reconquest and expansion into the Americas. Outside the boundaries of the Empire, the Hungarians, Poles, Czechs, Slovaks, Lithuanians, Croats and Slovenes formed their national identities at the same time that they accepted Catholicism. Much the same occurred with the Scandinavians and Russians, though we do not think of this because of their later defection. Even in lands long conquered by Islam, the Copts and other Christians of the Near East allow one the chance to see what Egypt and Syria were before that calamity.

Imagine, then, what may lie before our descendants! True enough, if we do our duty, the nearer future will see persecution; let not people be so preoccupied with the preservation of their remaining civil liberties that they lose sight of the greater importance of the immortal souls of themselves and those under their charge. But farther off, what are now mere potentials might have at last become real. Think of the regions of our country, with their ways and histories! New England and the South, the Midwest and Prairies, the Great Basin and the Northwest, all of them expressing together experiences of Catholicism that are as ingrained, organic, and natural, as anything in Jalisco, Brittany, or Sicily! We cannot, of course, know what the final result will be, in culture, economics, or politics, anymore than the Apostles could foresee what Christendom would produce. But we can know that the most important fruit of a Catholic civilization is the salvation of large numbers of souls—including, if we play our part, our own.

To say again, then, for us, patriotism means, first, *self-conversion*—the vision and practice of a Faith integrated with daily life. Whereupon follows evangelization—bringing our fellow citizens what they need both in this life and the next. Our failure to do so, or their failure to receive it, will endanger this country no end. It were well to conclude with words of Orestes Brownson earlier quoted:

> Time was when I paraded my Americanism, in order to repel the charge that an American cannot become a convert to the Church without ceasing to feel and act as an American patriot. I have lived long enough to snap my fingers at all charges of that sort. I love my country, and, in her hour of trial, I and my sons, Catholics like myself, did our best to preserve her integrity, and save her Constitution; and there is no sacrifice in my power that I would not make to bring "my kinsmen after the flesh" to Christ; but, after all, the Church is my true country, and the faithful are my real countrymen. Let the American people become truly Catholic and submissive children of the Holy Father, and their Republic is safe; let them refuse and seek safety for the secular order in sectarianism or secularism, and nothing can save it from destruction (*Brownson's Quarterly Review*, January 1873, pp.2-3).

BIBLIOGRAPHY

Part I

Bocca, Geoffrey, *Kings Without Thrones*, New York: The Dial Press, 1959.

Delaney, Edward D., *False Freedom*, Los Angeles: Standard Publications, 1954.

Doder, Dusko, *The Yugoslavs*, New York: Random House, 1978.

Foot, M.R.D., *Resistance: European Resistance to Nazism 1940-1945*, New York: McGraw-Hill, 1977.

Gayre, Robert, of Gayre and Nigg, *A Case For Monarchy*, Edinburgh: The Armorial, 1962.

Glaser, Kurt, *Czecho-Slovakia: A Critical History*, Caldwell: The Caxton Printers, 1961.

Hoehling, A.A., *Home Front, USA.*, New York: Thomas Y. Crowell, 1966.

Hoopes, Roy, *Americans Remember the Home Front*, New York: Hawthorn Books, 1977.

Jacobsen, Hans-Adolf, *July 20, 1944: Germans Against Hitler*, Bonn: Federal Press and Information Office, 1972.

Korbonski, Stefan, *Fighting Warsaw*, New York: Funk and Wagnalls, 1968.

Lees, Michael, *The Rape of Serbia*, New York: Harcourt Brace Jovanovich, 1990.

Miksche, Lt. Col. F.O. *Danubian Federation*, Camberley: privately published, 1953.

Miksche, Lt. Col. F.O. *Unconditional Surrender–The Roots of a World War III*, London: Faber and Faber, 1952.

Nicholls, George Heaton, *South Africa in My Time*, London: Jonathan Cape, 1962.

Nowak, Jan, *Courier From Warsaw*, Detroit: Wayne State University Press, 1982.

Oliveira, Plinio Correa de, *Nobility and Analagous Traditional Elites in the Allocutions of Pius XII*, York, PA: Hamilton Press, 1993.

Petrie, Sir Charles, *Monarchy in the 20th Century*, London: Andrew Dakers, Ltd., 1952.

Piekalkiewicz, Janusz, *The Cavalry of World War II*, New York: Stein and Day, 1980.

Ready, J. Lee, *Forgotten Allies*, Jefferson, NC: McFarland and Co., 1985.

Ready, J. Lee, *Forgotten Axis*, Jefferson, NC: McFarland and Co., 1984.

Rhodes, Anthony, *The Vatican in the Age of Dictators*, New York: Holt, Reinhart & Winston, 1973.

Schlabrendorff, Fabian von, *The Secret War Against Hitler*, New York: Pitman Publishing Corp., 1965.

Schoenbrunn, David, *Soldiers of The Night: The Story of the French Resistance*, New York: E.P. Dutton, 1980.

Snyder, Dr. Louis L., *Encyclopedia of the Third Reich*, New York: Paragon House, 1989.
Tomasevich, Jozo, *The Chetniks*, Stanford, CA: Stanford University Press, 1975.
Viorst, Milton, *Hostile Allies: FDR and De Gaulle*, New York: Macmillan, 1965.
Wedemeyer, Albert C., *Wedemeyer Reports!*, New York: Henry Holt and Co., 1958.

Part II

Blanshard, Paul, *American Freedom and Catholic Power*, Boston: Beacon Press, 1949.
Gadney, Reg, *Cry Hungary*, New York: Atheneum, 1986.
Goldman, Eric F., *The Crucial Decade*, New York: Vintage Books, 1956.
Hurley, Bishop Mark J., *The Unholy Ghost*, Huntington: Our Sunday Visitor, 1992.
Kirk, Russell, *The Conservative Mind*, Chicago: Henry Regnery Company, 1953.
Meisel, James H., *The Fall of the Republic: Military Revolt in France*, Ann Arbor: University of Michigan, 1962.
Meyer, Karl E., *The New America*, New York: Basic Books, 1961.
Miller, Douglas T., and Nowak, Marion, *The Fifties*, Garden City: Doubleday, 1977.
Neff, Donald, *Warriors at Suez*, New York: Simon and Schuster, 1981.
O'Neill, William L., *Coming Apart*, Chicago: Quadrangle Books, 1971.
Osman, Percy, *Space History*, New YorkL St. Martin's Press, 1983.
Lord Percy of Newcastle, *The Heresy of Democracy*, Chicago: Henry Regnery Company, 1955.
Robinson, Carol, *My Life With Thomas Aquinas*, Kansas City: Angelus Press, 1992.
Sulzberger, C.L., *The Test: De Gaulle and Algeria*, New York: Harcourt, Brace, & World, 1962.